Praise for *Lessons from the E-Front*

"Reading *Lessons from the E-Front* won't make you rich, bu might help you figure out the next step. At the very le you'll get a glimpse into the minds of e-commerce p neers—the ones destined to make it and the ones with t arrows in their backs."

—Larry Magid, syndicated columnist, *Los Angeles Tim*

"No longer will a cool idea and a PowerPoint presentatior be enough to get your business off the ground. If you wani to build a real business that lasts, read this book."

—Tom Taulli, Internet stock analyst, Internet.com

"The dot-com boom may be over, but the lessons from it endure. *Lessons from the E-Front* is full of valuable advice. Anybody looking to start a company should read this book."

—Andy Wang, founder, Ironminds.com,
and features editor, *GEAR* magazine

"Anyone who thinks high-tech business operates on a wing and a prayer will be enlightened by this book. Open it to any page and you're certain to glean a diamond-cut nugget of hard-won insight."

—Brad Hill, author, *Getting Started in Online Personal Finance*

"Matt Ragas was one of the first investment writers to realize that the New Economy is about more than just technology— it's about how companies use technology, whatever their business."

—Spencer Reiss, vice president, Gilder Publishing,
and co-editor, *New Economy Watch*

LESSONS FROM THE E-FRONT

50 TOP BUSINESS LEADERS REVEAL THEIR
HARD-WON WISDOM ON BUILDING A
SUCCESSFUL HIGH-TECH ENTERPRISE

MATTHEW W. RAGAS

PRIMA VENTURE
An Imprint of Prima Publishing
3000 Lava Ridge Court • Roseville, California 95661
(800) 632-8676 • www.primalifestyles.com

© 2001 by Matthew W. Ragas

PRIMA VENTURE and colophon are trademarks of Prima Communications Inc. PRIMA PUBLISHING and colophon are trademarks of Prima Communications Inc., registered with the United States Patent and Trademark Office.

Library of Congress Cataloging-in-Publication Data

Ragas, Matthew W.
    Lessons from the e-front : 50 top business leaders reveal their hard-won wisdom on building a successful high-tech enterprise / Matthew W. Ragas.
        p. cm.
    Includes index.
    ISBN 0-7615-2931-4
    1. High technology industries—Management. 2. New business enterprises—Management. 3. Success in business. I. Title: Lessons from the e-front. II. Title.

HD62.37 .R34 2001
658—dc21   2001021413

01 02 03 04 05 HH 10 9 8 7 6 5 4 3 2 1
Printed in the United States of America

How to Order
Single copies may be ordered from Prima Publishing, 3000 Lava Ridge Court, Roseville, CA 95661; telephone (800) 632-8676 ext. 4444. Quantity discounts are also available. On your letterhead, include information concerning the intended use of the books and the number of books you wish to purchase.

Visit us online at www.primalifestyles.com

To God, my family, and the Internet community at large. None of this would have been possible without you.

CONTENTS

FOREWORD

A RELIGIOUS, POLITICAL, AND BUSINESS REVOLUTION TOOK PLACE, and nobody had to die. The Internet provided us with the means to connect believers, democratize bad governments, and create a meritocracy in an expanding economy.

In 1993, Draper Fisher Jurvetson made the first investment in an Internet startup. It was called Internet Software and allowed people to buy and sell things over the Web. It was sold (a little early) to the Home Shopping Network for $5 million, possibly a thousandth of what it is worth today.

In 1996, Jack Smith and Sabeer Bhatia, two twenty-six-year-olds, came into our office with an idea for free e-mail on the Web. (Incidentally, this was their second idea. Their first was for a Web-based database. My partners, John Fisher and Steve Jurvetson, pulled the e-mail idea out of them after dismissing the database idea). Our partnership thought it was just nutty enough to work, and we invested a small amount of money to see where they could go with it. When Jack Smith announced (within two months of funding) that the product was up and running, I asked how they would market it. They suggested billboards and radio. I asked if there was some way for them to get the word out to all those people on the Web. They were horrified at the thought, saying, "That is spamming!" I then suggested that they put a trailer on each e-mail that said, "P.S. I love you. Get your free e-mail at Hotmail." Hotmail's founders began wondering at this point how it was, with all the venture capitalists in the world, that Draper Fisher Jurvetson was the group who said yes to their idea. After continuing to press, I finally wore them down to the point where they said, "Okay, but no 'P.S. I love you.'" I was thrilled. Within 18 months there were 11 million Hotmail users. More remarkably, CEO Sabeer Bhatia sent one e-mail to a friend in India, and within three weeks we had 100,000 registered Hotmail users in India. Steve and I coined this phenomenon "viral marketing," and we began to apply it to all our other companies.

Through our experiences in funding these two companies, we at Draper Fisher Jurvetson knew that the Internet would change the world. Not only could people do commerce on the Web, but ultimately everyone would be able to reach everyone else on the planet, and thus break through religious, governmental, and business impediments. China, India, Pakistan, and Africa could overcome religious feuds, corrupt governments, and economic barriers as they participate in this great equalizer.

In the religious world, it took 6,000 years to recruit 900 million Taoists, 3,000 years to recruit 20 million Jews, and 1,975 years to recruit 400 million Christians, for compound annual growth rates (CAGR) of between 0.34 percent and 1.74 percent. In seven short years the Internet recruited 200 million converts, for a CAGR of 1,493 percent. The Internet has brought people together in a way no religion has. People with different languages, cultures, races, and time zones are communicating like best friends.

STIFLING GOVERNMENTS HAVE BEEN CIRCUMVENTED AS THE Internet has grown. Eventually, I can imagine the Internet developing a competing government in cyberspace. While defense, highways, and other land-based government services would probably continue as inefficient monopolies, I can envision people choosing their social security programs, welfare safety nets, medicare, and educational systems all out in cyberspace. Let's face it, the computer is the ultimate bureaucrat—unemotional, fair, consistent, and completely without creativity.

In business, the opportunity is vast. The current world economy includes about 500 million people and represents about $20 trillion in products and services. If we connect the whole world, that number could conceivably increase tenfold. The opportunity breeds a meritocracy, where all the net new wealth is created by the people who build out this new world economy. Ultimately, they are the entrepreneurs.

These entrepreneurs generate unbridled creativity as the world adopts a piece of the Silicon Valley culture that I call "the equity economy." In the Silicon Valley today, an entrepreneur can get his rent paid, his legal work done, his P.R., his advertising, his investment banking, all his employees, and his cash (from a venture capitalist) all by using equity in his company. It has gotten to the point where people can buy a McDonald's cheeseburger for a partial share of Yahoo! This equity economy has additional benefits. Where a debt holder or an employee will generally be interested just in being paid, an equity holder is on the team. His interest is completely aligned with the interest of the company. He wants the company to succeed and become valuable. He becomes a promoter of the company.

So what is the downside here? Ultimately, there isn't one if it plays out this way, but for it to work (much like what Jefferson said about democracy), people have to be educated. The United States has become the economic powerhouse of the world, but we are 28th in math and science. While California has become the economic powerhouse of the United States, we are 49th in math and have a high school drop-out rate of 33 percent, which is similar to most Third World countries.

Education drives prosperity, and a lack of education drives the reverse. A high school drop-out has the likelihood of becoming a criminal, needing welfare, and needing a disproportionate share of medical attention. Conversely, a person well-educated in math and science has the likelihood of being a driver of growth in the economy.

The Silicon Valley has an interesting dilemma. While the economy is exploding so that jobs are being created at a tremendous rate, education has failed to provide the people with the tools needed to fill those jobs. For a capitalist, it is not difficult to see that the market has been stifled by a bureaucracy that is not fulfilling the needs of the society.

Nevertheless, society will be highly driven by the apocalypse that is the Internet. While companies' worth grows exponentially, the number of companies also grows exponentially, so it is hard for an investor to get his hands around what is happening. The original optimism of Wall Street for the Net came apart over a judge's ruling on Microsoft that essentially said to entrepreneurs, "Become successful, but not too successful or we'll ruin your life forever." My fear is that the United States government doesn't understand the possibility of competitive governance and will get in the way of

Internet progress. Perhaps the New Economy will have to take its businesses elsewhere, leaving this wonderful country with a culture of need rather than opportunity.

Given this as background, *Lessons from the E-Front* provides would-be entrepreneurs with the tools they need to become successful. Whether they are inventing fusion energy or promoting a new peer-to-peer network, whether they are planning their first sale or planning a new society, this book serves as a guidebook to plot their course through cyberspace.

—Tim Draper

INTRODUCTION

Mapping the E-Business Landscape
with the Next Economy Architects

TOUGH QUESTIONS DESERVE TOUGH ANSWERS.

So stop hiding under the covers and face reality for a change. Stare the Old Economy bogeyman in the face. Laugh at him. You're a survivor, while he's still destined to become an ancient relic.

Remember: The Internet isn't dead. Your business isn't either—at least not yet.

Forget what you've ever been told, that all good things must eventually come to an end. That nothing lasts forever. These are the hollow slogans of people who have always been afraid to embrace change. Routine and habit are their best and only friends. But business as usual will still die regardless of how many market pundits might say otherwise.

The real battle between optimists and skeptics has yet to be fought. For skeptics, the initial public offering of Netscape Communications in 1995 marked the true beginning of the New Economy dream bubble only to then be quickly popped with the April 2000 crash of the NASDAQ stock market. The dot-com bandits had been defeated. The Old Economy had remained king of the hill.

If only the real business world was this simplistic.

Perhaps the greatest explanation of the digital landscape of today already lies 30,000 years in our past. Only back then, the Old Economy was the strong and powerful Neanderthal man and the New Economy was the smaller and more agile Cro-Magnon man.

While the Neanderthals lived in small groups and rarely partnered with outsiders, the Cro-Magnons organized hunts and planned ahead in the anticipation of future events. Neanderthals existed for thousands of years, but eventually exhausted their food supplies in many regions of the world and withered away.

Like the wooly mammoth, the saber-toothed tiger, and the mastodon, the Neanderthal man was unable to adapt to a rapidly changing environment and died. On the other hand, the Cro-Magnon man anticipated these changes and thrived. The battle between Old Economy and New Economy companies will end up no different.

Those hyper-change companies who quickly adapt and locate new food sources in the marketplace will survive, while traditional firms who stubbornly remain fixated on existing business practices will eventually starve to death. The market will no longer need them and they will be discarded. History is indeed poised to repeat itself.

However, the leaders that will eventually emerge from the violent intersection of these two disparate digital and analog worlds will be neither Old Economy nor New

Economy in nature. Much like the Cro-Magnons who eventually evolved into modern man, the leaders of the New Economy will lay the foundation for a new digital landscape called the Next Economy.

With this in mind, I set out to write a book that Next Economy investors, entrepreneurs, executives, and workers could all use as a handbook for navigating this new digital landscape. Far from getting hung up on ivory tower theories, *Lessons from the E-Front* gets down in the trenches and provides clear actionable steps in major focus areas for Next Economy success.

Thus, in my mission to provide only proven and first-hand Next Economy tactics and strategies, I interviewed fifty successful entrepreneurs and senior executives for this book. These are many of the select few who have already successfully looked the Old Economy hurricane in the eye and won. For the first time ever, they are now sharing their own insights on how to play this game and win.

The opportunity for entrepreneurs to still create market-leading companies with an innovative value proposition initially hidden in a garage or musty basement has never been greater. At the same time, the opportunity for established companies to shed many of their obsolete business practices and emerge as true Next Economy leaders has never been greater.

The only real constant in the current digital business environment is that those individuals and companies that don't try something new are bound to eventually fail. Don't fall into one of these categories. Read this book. Take notes. Question the very fundamentals of your own business.

Then go out and change the world. It's waiting for you!

LESSONS FROM THE E-FRONT

CHAPTER 1

INSIDE THE EYE OF THE HURRICANE: IDEA CREATION AND BRAINSTORMING

TRADE IN YOUR RUNNING SHOES FOR A COMPASS AND WALKING stick. The race for the next new, new thing invariably begins as a sprint but often turns into a drawn-out marathon on a long road full of obstacles. Rarely ever does the billion-dollar idea that you suddenly had late at night with a couple of groggy friends seem as can't-miss and risk-free the next day. Successful idea creation doesn't work that way. Business isn't that easy.

Rarely does a great business idea hatched late on a Friday night generate millions in sales by Monday morning. Show me one example where this has been the case. Mark Andreessen and Jim Clark didn't develop the idea of a commercial "Web browser" one day and become billionaires the next. It just doesn't work that way. The successful idea-creation process takes time, patience, hard work, and a little luck. That doesn't mean, however, that entrepreneurs and companies can't follow a systematic framework to significantly improve their chances of successful brainstorming sessions.

As I'll show you in this chapter, there are a number of easy-to-follow steps that startups, as well as existing companies, can take to help separate unique new business ideas from run-of-the-mill, "me-too" concepts that today plague much of the technology world. Keep in mind, however, that even a unique new idea isn't necessarily a surefire homerun in the marketplace. In this section we will explore how entrepreneurs and executives can examine an idea to see if it is significantly superior to the competition and if it has the staying power to travel down multiple paths to success.

As we journey through this brainstorming and idea-creation process, you'll receive firsthand guidance from tech executives such as Harry Motro, the former CEO of Infoseek, Chris MacAskill of MightyWords.com, and iPrint.com founder Royal Farros. Next, serial entrepreneur Michael Rosenfelt will provide you with some core principles for leveraging technology into your new idea.

Tumbleweed founder Jeffrey Smith and PurchasePro.com chief Junior Johnson will follow up with advice on what entrepreneurs must do to successfully cross the finish line with their new ideas. Finally, Jeet Singh of Art Technology shares his lessons for continually improving existing ideas in the market. After all, new ideas don't stay "new" for very long unless a company continues to improve its products and services.

Know and Love Your Own Product

Okay, you're sitting at your cramped desk or cluttered workbench desperately looking for that spark to the next great business idea, but you have no clue how to begin. Here's a big hint: Create a product or service that you would know and love. I'm serious. Build something that gets you tremendously excited and your blood flowing.

If this brainstorming doesn't result in a new idea that has you thinking about it twenty-four hours a day, then you're doing something seriously wrong. Scrap that idea and start over. That's your gut saying you don't truly believe in this new product or service. That it's no good. In fact, it's downright dangerous.

The best ideas should always result in entrepreneurs or executives wanting to be martyrs if need be for their new product or service. Don't wince or cringe. That's what it takes to succeed with idea creation: undying passion. Unless you feel that sudden spark, a pack of well-funded companies or hungry entrepreneurs will trample your idea before it ever makes its way to market.

But if you do feel that passion deep in your gut, ask yourself this question: Would you really eat your own dog food? If your answer is a resounding yes—that you'd scarf down your new product or service quicker than a pit bull devours a can of dog food—then you're on the right track. See, as Harry Motro explains, the best and most enduring ideas are often created by people building products and services for themselves.

HARRY MOTRO

Chairman of MotroVentures; former Chief Executive Officer of Infoseek/GO.com

Q **Ragas:** Companies are always looking for advice on new ways to approach the idea-creation process. What lessons have you learned about successful idea creation in the information technology industry?

A **Motro:** People who are building products for themselves come up with the best ideas and start the best companies. The founding group has an intrinsic knowledge and passion for an opportunity, because they feel it in their gut. Music file-sharing company Napster is a perfect example. Founder Sean Fanning built Napster because he wanted to share music files. When I started CNN.com within Turner Broadcasting, it was because I loved the news, and I saw an opportunity to share information on the Net. I'm also the chairman of a company called Digete, which allows technical people to develop software using the Internet. The founders of the company were all at Whipro, which is the biggest Indian outsourcing company. They left there and went to a smaller company where they were helping their customers develop software, but the whole repetitive process of coordinating everyone frustrated them. So they built this new product and company based on a process that they know intrinsically, because they lived it for fifteen years. They're solving a problem that's in their gut. That's how a great product and company were created!

> *"People who are building products for themselves come up with the best ideas and start the best companies."*

Don't Let Focus Groups Decide Your Future!

Now that you've created the groundwork for a new product or service that you intrinsically know and would unabashedly use, it is important to survey the market's current landscape. Notice that I'm not suggesting that entrepreneurs start off the idea-creation process by surveying the market first. Focus groups, market researchers, and other information sources take too much time and should never be the starting points for good ideas. Going this route almost ensures that you will miss your market opportunity. Chasing the train that has left the station is never fun and for the most part is a waste of time.

Once an idea is created, however, focus groups and market researchers can serve an important role in the early stage of the development process. While neither of these sources will help you propose solutions and directly create new ideas, they can help you in defining existing and upcoming problems in the marketplace.

In other words, primary and secondary research are useful means to determine if the idea you're nurturing can become a product or service that the market will adopt if it knows that it will soon exist. A prime example of how to properly utilize research in the idea-creation process was related by Apple Computer founder Steve Jobs to MightyWords.com chief and former Apple employee Chris MacAskill.

CHRIS MACASKILL

Founder and Chairman of FatBrain.com; Chief Executive Officer of MightyWords.com

Q **Ragas:** There are many ways to approach the idea-creation process. Companies today often use focus groups, market researchers, and industry reports to aid them in the process. What advice do you have for companies and entrepreneurs on this aspect of the idea-creation process?

A **MacAskill:** I am somewhat influenced by the two years that I spent working for Steve Jobs at Apple Computer. A story that he told me maybe a dozen times went back to when Apple was making the Apple II computer, and the company was wondering how to react to IBM and Compaq's roll-out of MS-DOS–compatible computers. So Apple did a whole bunch of consumer research, which included focus groups. The customers unanimously said they wanted a DOS-compatible computer from Apple. A lot of people at Apple also wanted to do that, but Apple was afraid it could never make money with DOS, since it was becoming a commodity business. Steve Jobs then told me that the important thing to take away from the focus group is not what the customer says, it is figuring out what the customer's problem really is!

"The important thing to take away from the focus group . . . is figuring out what the customer's problem really is!"

Customers don't know you can build a Macintosh computer. They don't know about bit-map displays and other technology advancements. Consumers won't know that these products or services are even possible unless you put them right in front of them. Then, if the products and services really solve their problems, they'll like them. Companies need to remember that customers in a focus group can't tell them what they don't know. So watch out for focus groups.

Be Your Own Best Customer

Once research has indicated there will likely be a demand in the market for your new idea, the next thing to consider is how your new product or service will stack up when compared to the competition. A new idea that is only marginally better than existing solutions on the market should be marked dead on arrival. In fact, even an idea that seems three to five times better than existing solutions should probably be directed immediately to the nearest garbage dump.

Like iPrint founder and CEO Royal Farros, I remain a strident believer that unless your new idea literally annihilates the competition and immediately blows the socks off potential customers, you are probably wasting your time. Human beings are creatures of habit. Unless I can clearly see that your new idea makes an existing product or service seem like it is trapped in the Stone Age, I am going to continue to consume the old product. In other words, blow me away with your new idea or head immediately back to "GO" and try again.

ROYAL P. FARROS

Chairman, Founder, and
Chief Executive Officer of iPrint, Inc.

Q **Ragas:** What are the steps that a new or existing company should take to know it's heading down the right path towards creating a new killer product or service?

A **Farros:** You must first be your own best customer. If you are your own best customer, you are going to know when you create something really useful. It's important for companies to ask two pertinent questions. One: Am I a representative customer? Two: What is the competition? Maybe there are already similar solutions on the market, and your company's product or service is just reinventing the wheel.

Q **Ragas:** Okay. Entrepreneurs and executives need to start off by creating products or services that they would immediately use themselves. Generally, that's not so difficult to accomplish. What are additional guidelines that business people can follow during the idea-creation process?

A **Farros:** Entrepreneurs next have to ask themselves additional questions. Does the product or service save you time? Does it save you money? Can you improve your product or service an entire magnitude? This is very important, because making a product or service only five times better than the existing competition is not enough. Consumers by nature are like mice in a maze trying to find cheese. When consumers are trying to get the cheese, they don't mind taking the long route, because they are familiar

"If you are your own best customer, you are going to know when you create something really useful."

with that path and they don't have to learn anything new. Unless your new product or service offers ten times the amount of cheese, your potential customers will keep going after the moldy old cheese in the maze!

It's a Beautiful Thing If It's Faster, Better, Smarter!

At the end of the day, very few ideas improve a product or service by an entire magnitude or more. If your new idea has managed to leap over this high hurdle, then the next step in the idea-creation process is to fully explore how your idea is leveraging the inherent efficiencies of the Net or other technology advancements. This step is especially crucial because, unless an idea is leveraging some technological advantage to do things faster, smarter, and better, the chances of the competition eating this idea alive are very likely.

In essence, an idea that is able to weave itself into the fabric of the Web or related technology advancements is indeed a "beautiful thing," as Powered founder Michael Rosenfelt calls it. Great new ideas today must have some proprietary technological leverage in their process, otherwise the idea's foundation will erode and crumble over time. An idea that uses only brute force and sheer perseverance to create a paper-thin house of cards is easily toppled by predatory copycat companies. So find an idea rooted in a defensible proprietary technological edge or pack up your idea tent and go back and do additional homework.

MICHAEL ROSENFELT

Founder of Powered, Inc.; Venture Partner,
Impact Venture Partners

Q **Ragas:** Having started multiple successful technology companies, do you have any guidelines or ground rules for entrepreneurs who are looking to uncover truly successful and unique new business ideas?

A **Rosenfelt:** From a business perspective, all great new ideas come from identifying pain in the marketplace. Companies must find the pain that customers feel and then look for solutions. It sounds somewhat simplistic, but listening to customers and their needs, wants, and wishes is usually how companies get their best ideas. Successful idea creation is all about listening to customers tell what's causing constant pain and discomfort in their lives and then finding ways to solve their problems.

> *"Does your new idea truly allow the medium to do things faster, smarter, and better for your customers?"*

Q **Ragas:** In other words, companies must open their ears and listen to what their customers are telling them. They must find out where the real pain points and discomfort zones exist for their customers. What else is key to successful idea creation?

A **Rosenfelt:** An entrepreneur must create a new business idea so the target market can immediately see it is a beautiful thing. I say, "It's a beautiful thing," because the Net allows you to do things that you could not do before it existed. So companies need to ask themselves some questions about their new ideas. Can your new product or service bridge disparate communities and marketplaces? Can your product or service create greater efficiency than was there before? In other words, does your new idea truly allow the medium to do things faster, better, and smarter for your customers? Preferably, your idea should be all three. To the extent that you and your company can find new ideas that allow you to do that, you'll know you've indeed found a very beautiful thing!

Stay Stubborn and Focused

Even new ideas that are rooted in firm technological advantage don't necessarily see the light of day in the marketplace right away. See, that's the big secret that most successful entrepreneurs don't often share. Successful ideas are like planting tiny seeds in the ground. They take lots of tender loving care to nurture and grow. Even with all the fertilizer in the world, your idea is not going to grow to the heavens overnight.

In fact, more often than not, your little sapling is going to have to endure weeklong rain storms, hurricane force winds, severe heat, and everything else that Mother Nature—or in this case, the marketplace—can throw at it! So be prepared to dig in and weather this rocky period. The best nurturers of a new idea are those entrepreneurs and companies who stay incredibly stubborn and focused on the execution of their idea through thick and thin.

I'm not kidding. Throw all that you may have heard about the most successful entrepreneurs having "vision" right out the window. Bill Gates and Steve Ballmer didn't build Microsoft by sitting on vision "autopilot" for the past twenty-five years. Vision is nice, but at this stage of the game what really separate the winners from the losers in Idea Creation 101 are the executives and entrepreneurs who have incredible tenacity.

As Tumbleweed founder 〉 cessful software entrepreneur smith points out, a suc- BroadVision succeeded for the m. Pehong Chen of verance and tenacity—not vision. Wt because of perse- you to give up on your idea, that's whe everyone is telling time. Perseverance is what separates the becomes crunch doer. As the idea shepherd, it is your job to mer from the ever. The word "no" can simply not be in you harder than when you know you have a winner on your han cabulary faith. The best idea can move mountains even when no Have but you believes in it. ne

JEFFREY SMITH

Founder, Chief Executive Officer, and
President of Tumbleweed Communications

Q **Ragas:** What have you found to be the most challenging part of the entire idea-creation process that entrepreneurs must overcome to succeed with a new product or service?

A **Smith:** The challenging part of the idea-creation process is being tenacious enough and having enough courage to execute against your vision. The fact is, when you're starting a business, it's a roller coaster. Startup companies are not insulated from any of the ups, which can be incredible highs. You're also not insulated from the lows, which can be devastating at times! More than anything else, though, it's not just about having that great idea; companies must have the courage and tenacity to pursue it. The entrepreneur I would use as an example is Pehong Chen, the founder of BroadVision, a company that started in 1995 and was building an operating system for television set top boxes. That's not at all what BroadVision does today. BroadVision originally built an operating system for your television set. Today,

"The key to successful idea creation is being stubborn and focused at the same time!" wrong. They only cracked the code by being stubborn. It sounds obvious and somewhat silly, but it's true. The key to successful idea creation is being stubborn and focused at the same time!

Vision has over 500 Global 2000 customers and millions in sales. The company today sells Web software infrastructure tools. Their business now has nothing to do with the set top box. The truth is, the company's original vision was absolutely

Can Your Idea Travel Multiple Paths to Success?

I can't stress enough how essential it is for the keepers of new ideas to load up on "vitamin pills" of perseverance and tenacity as they attempt to bring their ideas to market. Yet even entrepreneurs and companies with the most undying passion and tenacity find ways to fail. I say "find ways to fail," because many ideas are created with only one narrow path to success in the market. Block that one path, and the entire business is toast.

As an idea shepherd, it's your job to develop an idea that can survive the turbulence and vicious twists and turns of the marketplace and head down multiple paths to success. Create paved and well-lit six-lane highways, because if your idea only targets one particular segment of the market and offers only one solution without any flexibility, you're begging for failure. The best ideas offer more than one narrow dirt path that the market can take to get from Point A to Point B.

This is a lesson that many online retailers like Boo.com, Beyond.com, and ValueAmerica were forced to learn first-hand during the spring of 2000. None of these companies had a backup plan to follow when the underlying econom-ics of their ideas proved not to be sound. Left with no wiggle room to rejuvenate their ideas, they were forced to walk off dejectedly to the nearest bankruptcy court.

However, a company can improve its chances for idea-creation success by not only creating multiple paths to the finish line, but also by surrounding itself with resourceful people, as PurchasePro.com chief Junior Johnson explains. Resourceful people understand that losing is not an option, so they are excellent at helping companies craft ideas that can follow multiple paths to success. If you do nothing else, remember to always craft ideas that allow your company to succeed even if your original path to market acceptance has been blocked.

CHARLES JOHNSON JR.

Founder, Chairman, and
Chief Executive Officer of PurchasePro.com

Q **Ragas:** We've all heard the phrase that good ideas are a dime a dozen. What can entrepreneurs and companies do to ensure that their ideas do, in fact, eventually succeed?

A **Johnson:** There are a couple of key areas that entrepreneurs must focus upon for successful idea creation. Number one is, How many different ways can you take your idea? Always keep in mind that a company or entrepreneur needs multiple paths to success within that same business. Most companies go down only one path, and if it's already blocked, they're screwed. The second key to successful idea creation is the willingness to be resourceful. It's more important to know what you don't know than to know what you do know. If you've got resourceful people and multiple paths for your idea, it's very, very hard not to be successful, because you've got people who absolutely are going to get to the finish line.

Q **Ragas:** You're getting right to the heart of the idea-creation process. Companies must realize that the best ideas today are the ones that can shift and head in different directions if need be. There must be a certain amount of flexibility from the beginning to the execution of any new business concept.

A **Johnson:** The truth is that most entrepreneurs and startup companies know they are going to be successful but don't know what direction their business is going to go to get there! I use a little saying, "If you wait until all the traffic lights are green, you will never leave your house." I believe there's a lot of truth to that! Losing is not an option. If losing is not an option, then you need a business idea that can go down multiple paths. Secondly, companies must surround themselves with flexible people who can think about going down other paths if the business suddenly changes.

"If losing is not an option, then you need a business idea that can go down multiple paths."

Let Your Customers Open the Gates to Product Innovations

At today's tremendous pace of rapid change and innovation, a new idea that looks shiny one day often seems tarnished and outdated a few months later. There's simply no time to pat yourself on the back when your new idea has been accepted in the marketplace. Continuing to build the next generation of products and services that are a magnitude above your company's existing ideas has become more crucial than ever before. No established idea is safe from obsolescence today.

Even companies that continue to innovate often look like they are running in place, while companies that live on the glory of past ideas are already out of the race. Thus, as an executive or entrepreneur, you must constantly be on the prowl for additional sources of idea inspiration. Don't know where to look? Often, the primary source of product or service innovation is dancing right under your nose.

That's right. Turn to your customers for guidance. Don't just ask them what they want, though. Get down and dirty and actually build a select number of custom products or services for your clients each year. With this knowledge in hand, you will be better able to gauge exactly what innovations and improvements you should add to additional products or services, as Art Technology founder Jeet Singh points out. Your customers are a gold mine of new ideas and additional innovations. Now get to work and start finding the nuggets.

JEET SINGH

Founder and Chief Executive
Officer of Art Technology Group

Q **Ragas:** We've already discussed some of the keys to successful idea creation. What advice and lessons do you have to share with companies who are approaching idea creation from the perspective of improving existing products and services?

A **Singh:** This is definitely our secret sauce. It's kind of funny, but I would say that we "lucked" or "unlucked" into becoming very good at the idea-creation process because we didn't have any money. Basically, our company was making anything that people asked us to build. So a customer would say, "Hey, would you build me an online Web service?" Little by little we realized that by doing services work we were receiving a whole lot of information showing us what to add to our existing products. We'd do this for about four or five customers per year, and then every two years we looked back at our products and said, "What should we add?" Usually, at least one of the service projects we'd done would turn into a mission statement, "Let's just build that again," and we'd add it to one of our existing products.

Q **Ragas:** By doing custom projects and additional services work for existing clients, companies are able to get a much better understanding of the features and improvements that should be added to the "next generations" of their existing products or services.

A **Singh:** Services work completely dictates where our product innovation goes. Our innovation process is very customer driven, but not just in asking customers what they want. The key is to actually build a few generations of products for customers over the years. By doing this, a company stores up a huge pantry of technology ideas and concepts that can be generalized very quickly. Then, a year later, a new product comes out. We've never had a crystal ball. People say visionary this and visionary that. I've never had a vision in my life! I'm just hoping a customer will tell our company what to build next. Existing companies will innovate well with fresh ideas as long as they keep in touch with what's going on with their customers!

"Existing companies will innovate well with fresh ideas as long as they keep in touch with what's going on with their customers!"

CHAPTER 2

BUILDING A SUCCESSFUL DIGITAL BUSINESS MODEL

A KILLER NEW PRODUCT OR SERVICE WITHOUT A WELL-THOUGHT-out business model is a lot like a sailor lost at sea without navigational charts. Think about it. Suppose we packed a dream team of yachtsmen onto a ship and told them to set sail and find a new route to Asia. Being pros, they'd give it their best shot, but without charts to guide their journey, they'd end up drifting the oceans endlessly. Eventually, they'd run out of supplies and more than likely not survive.

Companies that create innovative products or services without well-crafted business models act much the same way. They set off on their long journey into uncharted waters without packing the proper supplies or even hiring the right crew. Too many startups, and even established companies, believe they can succeed in the marketplace merely by throwing their new product or service over the side and hoping it will swim. A sink-or-swim approach to developing a business model is usually the next thing to committing suicide.

As you will see in this chapter, there are clear definable steps that a company can take to develop an e-business model around a new product or service. While one can never remove all of the risks and related hazards from a market opportunity, there are simple ways to lower the chances that your new idea as it sails along won't suddenly be attacked by marauding pirates. A well-crafted business model, though not impenetrable, does give Next Economy explorers the opportunity to begin their journey with a sturdy ship. Your company can hit the waters with an up-to-date chart and more than gut instincts to sail by!

To guide you in this process, I'll share with you the insights of a number of technology executives who have successfully set sail with a variety of technology-focused business models. First, Rare Medium founder Glenn Meyers steers us in the right mental direction, followed by former Infoseek CEO Harry Motro describing how to properly identify a customer's true pain points. Vicinity's Emerick Woods and CitySearch's Charles Conn will then provide additional insights into the business-model-creation process.

Next, Mark Walsh of VerticalNet tackles the consumer behavior side of the business-model equation, followed by PurchasePro.com founder Junior Johnson explaining the importance of building a profit-focused business from day one. Keeping in mind that even the most successful business model is constantly evolving, GoTo.com chief Ted Meisel shares with you the importance of remembering how your business is creating distinctive value. A business model that drifts away from how it is already creating distinctive value is a company off course and asking to be smashed up on the jagged rocks.

You Can't Flip a Business Like a Burger

The heady days of Net entrepreneurs starting companies built on far-out ideas and impossible growth projections in hopes of a quick sale to an unsuspecting and clueless larger company are history. Let's face it. The seemingly open-ended potential of the Internet simply isn't so new and alluring anymore. The days of slapping a dot-com onto the name of an existing business and watching its stock price soar to the moon already seem like ancient history. People aren't so naïve now. They've been burned and learned. Results—not potential—now reign supreme.

In the mid to late nineties, some entrepreneurs started tech companies simply to "flip" them like hamburgers a year or two later by selling them either to public markets or bricks and mortar companies. That game is over. The burger business is back where it belongs in fast food restaurants, not in the boardrooms and hallways of tech startups. Skepticism, not optimism, is what most tech entrepreneurs should now expect for their new ideas. Which means that unless you are committed to creating an incredibly compelling business model, this flipping game is not for you. Instead, I suggest you spruce up your old resume and go look for a nine-to-five job again.

As Rare Medium founder Glenn Meyers explains, half-baked business models with rookie management teams are dead. For the most part, Meyers is right. No matter how wonderful your new product or service might be, you as a tech entrepreneur must show potential customers from day one that you have the total package and are in this game for the long haul. If not, you're destined to fail. When I say the "total package," I mean a company that has a passionate and seasoned management team and a unique idea in an entirely new emerging market segment.

The first step in creating a new business model is to decide if your company even possesses all of the critical components to the total package that I just described. If your business doesn't bring this total package to the game, then it's time for you either to retool your entire company or go back to chapter one and begin the idea-creation process all over again.

GLENN MEYERS

Chief Executive Officer, Chairman,
and Founder of Rare Medium Group

Q **Ragas:** You've seen a number of interesting business models and concepts come across your desk. Based on your experience, what lessons can you offer to entrepreneurs looking to develop a winning business model?

A **Meyers:** The first thing is that you can't be in the burger business. If you're going to be in business just to "flip" a company, then you're going to get found out very early on. Those days are over! The idea that some corporate guy or young kid can start a business with the intention of flipping it to another larger, clueless company is thankfully history. The "give-it-all-up" mentality is now the first criterion. Without passion and commitment, don't even waste your time developing a business model! Even so, just meeting this first criterion doesn't mean that you will end up being successful.

Q **Ragas:** Exactly. Companies and entrepreneurs must realize that you can give 110 percent all day long, but if your company is competing in a crowded market with a lackluster business model, you're going to stay right at square one.

A **Meyers:** Right. The second criterion is that the business model has to be very, very unique, and it has to be in a space that is a couple of degrees ahead of today's standard deviation. There's just so much "me-too" stuff out there in the market. Companies must be focused on the next great thing!

Q **Ragas:** So the key to creating the next killer business model is all about catching the next big wave that no one else sees yet! Companies and entrepreneurs must develop solutions that are ahead of the curve and that the rest of the market hasn't even thought of yet.

A **Meyers:** Yes. I don't think you can sit and read a business magazine to find out what the next big wave is, either. It must be a unique business model in a unique market space that is just forming. That's

> *"If you're going to be in a business just to 'flip' a company, then you're going to get found out very early on."*

the second box to check off when creating a business model. The third criterion covers execution-oriented issues. Who's the management team? Who are the investors? Who's the board? Do the entrepreneurs have track records and experience? The idea of the "trust-me" kind of business model where friends and family fund the business because every next door neighbor is getting rich from investing in tech companies is over also!

Are You a Painkiller or a Vitamin Pill?

If you've come to the conclusion that you already have the total package just described, then the next step in building a business model is to understand how your company is creating a true value proposition for your customers. Although this is easier said than done, it's not nearly as hard as it may appear. First off, a company can always create a winning value proposition and a compelling business model by successfully identifying customers' pain points.

Once you've identified your customers' aches, bruises, and other ailments, you will be able to devise a business model built upon a value proposition that we'll call either a painkiller or a vitamin pill. As ex-Infoseek head Harry Motro explains, painkillers are solutions that heal existing pain points for customers, whereas vitamin pills solve problems customers may not even know they have, yet make them feel healthier and more efficient.

Web-hosting giant Exodus Communications is a prime example of a company whose business model is focused on being a super-charged vitamin pill. When technology companies out-source their Web-hosting operations to Exodus as a third party, they save significant time and money, as well as precious techni-cal resources. In essence, Exodus' clients feel much "healthier," because they have become far more technically efficient.

On the other hand, online exchange companies like FreeMarkets and PurchasePro.com are good examples of companies that have created painkillers at the core of their business models. Both these companies capitalized on the fact that organizations need to simplify the process and to lower costs connected with the purchase of their supplies and raw materials. By offering straightforward solutions to ease this purchasing pain, FreeMarkets and Purchase.Pro.com have made a niche for themselves in the marketplace.

While I can't decide for you which path your company should choose, I can point out that vitamin pills generally offer a company the largest overall market opportunity.

HARRY MOTRO

Chairman of MotroVentures;
former Chief Executive Officer of Infoseek/GO.com

Q **Ragas:** What steps must companies take in the business-model-creation process after they have developed a new product or service?

A **Motro:** First, look at the customers for your product or serv-ice and try to understand how you are creating a true value proposition. The deeper a company or entrepreneur understands customers' needs and pain points, the easier it is to build a business model. Companies should divide business models into either painkillers or vitamin pills. Painkillers are the easier businesses to create. With painkiller models, there's an obvious set of pain, and your product or service is going to solve that pain. The customer will pay your company money to help remedy the cause of that pain, whatever it happens to be!

> *"Companies should divide business models into either painkillers or vitamin pills."*

Q **Ragas:** Okay. So companies must understand when they embark on creating a business model around their product or service how they are really creating a value proposition for their customers. They can then divide the customer's pain points into two separate models.

A **Motro:** Yes. The other type, the vitamin pill, is a business model that originates from talking to a potential customer and finding out the customer doesn't have any existing pain. As a company, you say, "I know you don't have any existing pain, but I'm going to make you feel better anyway. I'm going to make you feel this great thing you've never felt before." That's a harder business model to implement! When you offer a vitamin pill, your prospective customer has to take a little leap of faith. If he does, the upside can be even bigger for your company and you, the entrepreneur. You may grow a new market, and your company then has the potential to really own the market and build a brand around it!

Solve Problems That Are Already Reasonably Well-Defined

While identifying customer pain points is a great way to uncover your company's true value proposition to the marketplace, many times it's not just a strong value proposition inside your model that will get your sales moving. Like it or not, value is only visible to your customers if you wrap it up in a "package" that they can understand. Unfortunately, this simple concept entirely escapes many fledgling companies.

One need only take a glimpse at the current technology landscape to see that many digital companies are attacking the business-model-creation process as if the old rules of business still don't apply. As if tech companies are able to operate in a magic bubble of new economic principles. Don't believe this hollow rhetoric for a second. This bubble has already been popped if it ever existed in the first place. E-business companies must approach the business-model-creation process like any other industry.

All too often, I see digital companies create incredible new products or services, only to watch them flounder due to ill-conceived business models that fail to package solutions in ways their prospective customers understand. Improve the wheel. Don't try to reinvent it when creating your new business model.

Let's use a traditional all-American business like the corner ice cream store as an example. It just so happens that this store has won a national award for its delicious chocolate ice cream. Everyone knows that this little shop has the best ice cream in town. Yet the owner doesn't accept cash, the shop is only open two hours a day, and the ice cream is sold not in cones but in cups. Is it any surprise customers stay away and that the store fails in only a few weeks?

I'd like to think that no ice cream shop owner would be foolish enough to cripple the success of his product with these restrictions. Unfortunately, companies that don't invent business models around problems that are already reasonably well-defined by their customers and offer flexible solutions are very much like the bizarre ice cream shop. Always think simple. Tried and true is better than complex and untested. Look at Yahoo. Its many advertisers already understood the concept of targeting audiences on television and newspapers. Yahoo took this tried and true model and shifted it successfully to the Net.

As Vicinity CEO Emerick Woods points out, his wireless infrastructure service company also consciously created a business model that his customers would understand. Vicinity's pricing model is based on driving online customer leads into bricks and mortar stores. While this is not a glamorous business model by any means, it gets the job done. Vicinity has addressed a problem that is understood by the company's prospective customer base and has increased its own chances for long-term success in the process.

EMERICK WOODS

Chief Executive Officer and President of Vicinity; former Chief Executive Officer and President of TuneUp.com

Q **Ragas:** There are obviously a number of ways to go about crafting a successful business model. From your experience what should entrepreneurs and startup companies keep in mind when crafting a technology-focused business model?

A **Woods:** The first false assumption that companies often fall into is that somehow the basic rules of business and economics don't apply to the Internet. Many companies have fallen into the trap of thinking that somehow you can make money by selling a product for less than it costs to manufacture or a service for less than it costs to deliver. Entrepreneurs and companies need to always look at the underlying costs to deliver their end product or service and charge at a price point where they can make money. It sounds stupid. The number of times that I've talked to companies and they don't acknowledge this basic principle surprises me!

Q **Ragas:** At the end of the day, business online or offline is still about making money and posting profits for the company's shareholders. However, many technology companies are still not focused enough from the initial creation of their business model on how they plan to rapidly become cash-flow positive.

A **Woods:** The other lesson is that companies should not focus on the Internet as being some magical new paradigm. Instead, companies should attempt to develop business models that take the Internet and leverage the things it does really well against a set of problems that are already reasonably well understood by their prospective customers. That's why, in our case, our business model is all about driving customers' leads to physical stores. This is the kind of business model that the bricks and mortar companies have understood for a long time. A company succeeds when its business model is developed around a set of problems that are already reasonably well understood.

"Entrepreneurs and companies need to always look at the underlying costs to deliver their end product or service."

Leverage Technology's Core Advantages

Solving problems and pain points is great, but this is only one piece of the entire engine that must be developed for powering a killer business model. This engine must rest upon a firm technological foundation. As I stressed in chapter one, enduring new ideas and business models must contain some form of proprietary technological advantage. Business models that don't find ways to leverage the core advantages of the Net and other new technologies will find themselves running on only one cylinder.

Companies should not view new technologies like the Web and wireless networks simply as new means to achieve old ends.

That would be a waste of time. Using new technologies in this fashion is fine for short-term advancements for your business. But this type of mentality will not give your company any sustainable competitive advantage. As we've already seen played out dramatically in the stock market over the past two years, companies that simply attempt to "super-charge" existing business concepts online are at best short-term successes.

Scores of online retailers and new media startups have failed not because of a sudden shortage of capital but because these companies were not really leveraging their technological foundation's core advantages. They were simply tap dancing around in the same tired old costume. Slapping a traditional mail order catalog or literary magazine onto the Web and trying to build an enduring business may seem laughable today, but these feeble concepts were hailed as almost revolutionary just five short years ago.

Looking back, it is easy to see that technology was used in both these cases as a nifty new crutch rather than as a foundation for finding a new way to walk. Today's giant new wave of e-companies and entrepreneurs must work from the beginning to actively craft a business model that marries— not just flirts—with the technological advantages of the Net and related technologies. Learn the advantages and disadvantages of the medium inside and out, then find ways to use this special basket of core technological advantages as both a platform for solving your customers' problems and a defensible barrier against your competition.

CHARLES CONN

Former Chairman and Cofounder of
TicketMasterCitySearch.com

Q **Ragas:** While it's important that companies and entrepreneurs create business models that solve problems that are already reasonably well defined in the marketplace, there are other lessons that can be applied to creating a killer business model. What else should companies do?

A **Conn:** Companies need to develop business models that use the Web's capabilities and complementary technologies to do something in a different and better way from how it's been done before. So much of what companies are trying on the Web is to "electrify" a business that already exists. You saw that for example with online yellow pages companies. That business model didn't use the capabilities of the medium! Many online retailers also fit into this category of simply trying to "electrify" existing offline businesses. Where's the insight in that? There is none! Entrepreneurs and companies must use the Web for what it's good at.

Q **Ragas:** In other words, it's one thing to use technology as a platform for solving a problem that your customers already know exists, but your entire business model is a waste if it doesn't properly leverage the superior capabilities of this medium!

A **Conn:** When Internet entrepreneurs sit down to create a business model, they need to ask, What's the medium good at? The medium is good at serving up highly tailored information to individuals according to their preferences. Amazon.com is an example of a company that is very good at making personalized recommendations. The medium is also powerful because you can keep it up-to-date and very "fresh" with near real-time information or data. The medium allows incredible immediate interaction with your customers. If you're not leveraging these characteristics of the Web and related technologies into your company's business model, you're probably going to be messed up!

"Develop business models that use the Web's capabilities and complementary technologies to do something in a different and better way from how it's been done before."

Don't Try to Change Consumer Behavior

Leverage the core technologies of your business and even attempt to change the world with your company, but don't ever attempt to change existing consumer behavior. Companies that attempt to change consumer behavior are effectively marching their new product or service straight into a military firing line without even the protection of a bullet-proof vest. Save yourself and your company the misery. I know that it can seem financially tempting to whip up a business model that attempts to alter the existing behavior of consumers or corporations. Resist this urge, and you will live to fight another day. Chasing dollar signs by attempting to alter the behavior of human beings is one science experiment that your company is better off not trying.

Don't believe me? Look at the high-profile blowup of Priceline.com's WebHouse Club. This online shopping service allowed consumers to bid on grocery items, much like Priceline's very successful "name-your-price" airline ticket service. One can see how WebHouse appeared to be a multi-billion-dollar idea that consumers would love. But after months of tests and over $360 million in wasted venture capital, WebHouse came to the conclusion that its business model was seriously flawed.

What went wrong? There are a number of different hollow reasons that have been bandied about, but I firmly believe WebHouse flopped primarily because the company attempted to alter existing consumer behavior. Plain and simple. It just doesn't work. An overwhelming majority of the population was simply not ready to sit in front of a computer screen before each trip to the grocery store and bid on the price of paper towels. That's just not how human beings do things.

Keep this story in mind when you are developing your company's e-business model. Don't let your new product or service turn into the next WebHouse Club. VerticalNet chairman Mark Walsh takes this concept a step further through his description of a fictitious ultra-niche Internet startup called "DentalFloss.com." Clearly, many companies have confused themselves with the mistaken notion that being first in a particular sector gives them the leeway to devise a business model that goes against the grain of human transactional behavior.

Whatever the example given, though, be it WebHouse, DentalFloss.com, or another consumer-behavior-changing business model, my message remains essentially the same. It's fine and dandy to create a company that sets out to change the world. Just be sure to leave consumer behavior alone. Think of this area as being much like the third rail in the subway station. Leave it alone. Don't touch it, and it won't hurt you or your business. In other words, ride with human decision-making habits—not against them. Otherwise, you run the risk of your business being zapped right out of the marketplace.

MARK WALSH

Chairman of VerticalNet;
former Senior Vice President of America Online

Q **Ragas:** What are some of the pitfalls and traps that entrepreneurs and companies need to be sure to avoid when they embark on creating a successful business model?

A **Walsh:** There was this spasm of belief that the Internet would take over the world, and all the bricks and mortar stores we have enjoyed relationships with for centuries would all but disappear. We would go to the "dot-com" site of whatever product we were looking for to purchase our products. Wrong! My own sarcastic example is the hypothetical DentalFloss.com site where consumers would magically flock to register all of their dental floss needs! There was this mass fantasy fueled by a lot of venture capital money that made entrepreneurs believe they would be successful if they could come up with a catchy Web address and get to a category first. It was a misconception that Internet success was all about creating something like the next DentalFloss.com, which had the largest selection of dental floss in all different sizes and shapes, waxed and unwaxed!

> *"There was this mass hysteria that never considered that human beings really don't change!"*

Q **Ragas:** Right. Entrepreneurs and executives need to avoid the trap of creating business models that are solutions in search of a problem. Just because a new business can be created doesn't mean consumers are going to adopt that new product or service.

A **Walsh:** Yes. There was this gold-rush misconception among companies and entrepreneurs. They thought if you were out there first you could stake the biggest land claim. All you had to do was build the fences, get the horses and shovels, and you'd find the gold! There was this mass hysteria that never considered that human beings really don't change. We have not changed. No matter what technology becomes available, our transactional behavior does not change. We certainly gather more information on the Web before we conduct a transaction now, but basic transaction behavior hasn't changed for most products. Business models that attempt to change human behavior are bound to fail!

Is Your Business Built to Make Money from Day One?

Let's assume you've already identified your customers' primary pain points and developed innovative new solutions to existing problems that are already reasonably well defined.

At the same time, your company has wisely avoided the pitfall of attempting to alter existing human behavior. Next up on the business-model-creation process should be to focus on crafting a business model that contains a clear path to profitability from the outset. This should be a quick "show-me-the-money" game plan that is easy to understand and execute for your employees and your management team, as well as potential investors and even major customers.

This means a couple of things. First off, I'm quite serious when I say that every successful business model must have a clear path to profits right off the bat. The game of "acquire market share first, generate profits later" for your new product or service doesn't cut it anymore—if it ever did. "Later" has very quickly become "now." The motto should now be, "Acquire market share now, generate profits now." As a result, virtually every startup is now scrambling to reach breakeven and demonstrate that it can in fact generate real earnings. However, if more of these companies had developed a business model that actually worked from day one, they wouldn't have needed nearly as many layoffs and reorganizations to achieve this goal.

Sadly, a large slice of the digital world until very recently was built upon cash-happy dreams of rapidly taking companies public or flipping them to unsuspecting offline corporations or frothy tech companies. Now, with the capital markets having put an end to these shenanigans, the game has shifted to a more realistic playing field that rewards technology-focused companies that can show the same tried and true financial sanity as the traditional business world. A combination of impressive top-line revenue growth with strong earnings growth and sustainable gross margins is now what matters. As PurchasePro.com founder Junior Johnson points out, successful New Economy companies should be built to make money—not go public. Heed these words when you build your own business model, or you run the risk of becoming irrelevant to the market over the long haul.

CHARLES JOHNSON JR.

Founder, Chairman, and
Chief Executive Officer of PurchasePro.com

Q **Ragas:** Many companies and entrepreneurs are adept at creating what appear to be—on the surface at least—very impressive business models, but they lack a clear path to profitability. What advice can you share?

A **Johnson:** From day one, a technology company cannot only employ the visionary "dot-com mentality." Your business must have a combination of offline- and online-type business people. The company needs a blend of corporate world workers with entrepreneurial individuals to achieve a nice balance. One thing we've always done at PurchasePro is to take the top-line vision of an e-commerce company and the bottom-line vision of an offline company. Technology companies must never take their focus away from making a profit for their shareholders.

> *"Companies shouldn't be built to go public. They should be built to make money."*

We're not inhibiting our top-line growth, but at the same time we've been very, very sensitive to the profit factor from day one. Companies shouldn't be built to go public. They should be built to make money. At the end of the day, an entrepreneur must build a business model to make money, not to build the top line and try to figure out the bottom line later. I've seen far too many companies have great technology but not really understand what they are doing from a business perspective.

Beware of Tech Fads!

One of the biggest mistakes a successful company can make is to allow external pressures from the marketplace to alter an existing functional business model. I'm not telling you to entirely ignore the latest trends in your company's industry, but I am advising you to always approach a new trend with a skeptical eye. In other words, better safe than sorry. New-technology manias are easy to be sucked into and almost always seem alluring at first glance. After all, who doesn't want their company to be on the cutting edge? We all do. No company in today's competitive market likes to seem tentative and conservative to the outside world.

In fact, we've developed into a business culture where daring and dynamic "death-defying" companies seem to be richly rewarded by the media and shareholders—at least initially. Notice that I said initially—not long term. As in any business, short-term hype and glitz can be good for a few magazine articles and a temporarily sizzling stock price. However, these same parties will happily crucify you if by jumping on the latest technology fad, your company has thrown its business model badly off track. I would always much rather treat the latest technology mania like a ticking time bomb, not some wonderful new miracle elixir.

There is a relatively simple way for a company to make sure its business does not fall into this trap of "chasing a fad." First, ask yourself this important question: How is your company's product or service creating distinctive value? Once you have this answer, see if this new technology trend coming down the pike offers an obvious way to strengthen your existing distinctive-value-creation process. If the new trend would actually enhance your existing business, that's great. If not, you'll know you're not missing out on anything.

GoTo.com head Ted Meisel recounts for us a lesson he learned from the "push technology" fad of the mid nineties.

TED MEISEL

President and Chief Executive Officer of GoTo.com

Q **Ragas:** We've already discussed in detail the keys to creating the next killer business model. What do entrepreneurs and companies need to keep in mind when they have a business model that works, but they feel pressured by new trends to alter their existing formula?

A **Meisel:** It is really important for companies to stay focused on the way they create value and what makes them distinctive. A few years ago when I was working at CitySearch before joining GoTo.com, you may remember the "push" technology fad that occurred. This push fad came around very quickly, and we immediately dropped some pending deals at CitySearch to try and do push technology partnerships, because we felt pressure from the market to jump on the bandwagon. You know how that all turned out!

> *"Companies need to stay focused on what they do best and not what other people want them to do!"*

Q **Ragas:** Definitely. The push technology craze flamed out very quickly with a strong backlash from consumers. Many of these push companies either failed or had to drastically alter their businesses. It's difficult to do at times, but a successful company must remain true to its original business model.

A **Meisel:** Yes. The problem with "chasing the fad" for a business is that even if push technology had worked, we weren't creating any distinctive value at CitySearch with it. We were creating distinctive value at CitySearch by creating specific content about a city and a directory for local businesses. That was the value we were creating that was distinctive. If push technology had won, we could have worked with one or multiple push technology vendors. Companies need to stay focused on what they do best and not what other people want them to do!

CHAPTER 3

VULTURE CAPITALISTS AND OTHER MYSTICAL MONEYMEN

IF BUILDING A NEW BUSINESS IS A LOT LIKE THE APOLLO MISSION to put a man on the moon, then venture capital is the high-octane rocket fuel needed to shoot your startup into orbit. Contrary to popular belief, the modern day venture capitalist is not a new creation. Entrepreneurs have been turning to mystical moneymen as primary sources of risk capital for hundreds of years now. This is extremely important for entrepreneurs and executives to understand. While the sophistication of the risk capital game has drastically increased over the past few decades, the end goal of the venture investor and entrepreneur remains essentially the same: To create wealth for their shareholders. Lots of it.

Let's take a glance at the history books to see what I mean. Roughly 500 years ago, Spanish and Portuguese royalty invested heavily in the expeditions of swashbuckling, seafaring explorers in hopes of reaping huge financial returns in the forms of gold and rare spices. A hundred years later, the British monarchy funded explorers to set up lucrative fur-trading operations across Canada. And how can Americans forget about the Dutch and their venture-backed business ambitions? In 1621, a handful of Dutch investors formed the Dutch West India Company, which eventually purchased Manhattan Island from the Indians for trinkets valued at twenty-four dollars!

Christopher Columbus is another example of an entrepreneur struggling to raise venture capital for his business. Columbus attempted to gain sponsorship for his first voyage from Portugal, France, and England before Spain finally decided to back him. Only through persistence did Columbus manage to get his business off the ground. On his many journeys in search of a new route to the Indies, Columbus had to deal with shortages of supplies as well as a crew that was often near mutiny. If this story doesn't remind you of an entrepreneur of today trying to manage and grow a cash-strapped startup, then I don't know what does.

As you can see, the venture capital and risk-taking game has remained virtually the same for entrepreneurs over the centuries. Entrepreneurship has always been about high risk with high reward, and there has almost always been a third party willing to invest in a new idea or dream—be it European monarchy or a couple of venture capitalists on Sand Hill Road in Silicon Valley. This knowledge of history is particularly useful for entrepreneurs starting businesses today. Understanding that the risk capital game has not significantly changed over the years gives you a significant edge over the competition. Too many entrepreneurs and executives mistakenly believe that venture capital is a new and complicated game that can't be mastered even with proper preparation. They're wrong.

As I will show you in this chapter, there are in fact a series of steps entrepreneurs and executives can take to successfully navigate the tumultuous world of vulture capitalists and mystical moneymen. While there can be no guarantee that following these steps will result in your company becoming the next Oracle or Cisco, you'll almost undoubtedly be better prepared to interact with venture capitalists than before you read this chapter. As we begin, we'll receive firsthand insights on the preparatory side of the process from Jeet Singh of Art Technology, Dave Goldberg of Launch Media, and iPrint.com chief Royal Farros.

MightyWords founder Chris MacAskill and Mike Levy of Sportsline will then share the importance of receiving proper introductions into top-tier venture capital firms. Once you're in the door at a venture shop, you still need to find a way to close the deal. For this step in the process, we'll receive valuable guidance from Ventro founder Dave Perry and John Holt of the Cobalt Group. Finally, I'll delve into the world of alternate capital sources, such as angel investors, with the help of PurchasePro CEO Junior Johnson. It'll then be your job to hit the pavement, start pounding on doors, and create the next modern-day, high-tech equivalent of a successful fur, gold, and spice trading operation of centuries ago.

Welcome to the Venture Capitalist Mentality

While venture capitalists may be on the same playing field as an entrepreneur and have the same ultimate goal in mind, they are able to play by an incredibly more flexible set of rules. Think of the venture capitalist as a baseball player who never strikes out swinging. Sounds like a great game, doesn't it?

While moneymen do strike out a fair share of the time, that small detail is usually not recorded on the final scoreboard, or the internal rate of return for the investment fund. Instead, venture capitalists always attempt to knock the ball out of the park, because they are rewarded by the results they post for an entire season, not just one ballgame. Imagine base-ball slugger Mark McGwire always swinging for the fences, instead of worrying about his batting percentage. The job of venture capitalists is to constantly seek out outrageously high returns for their own investors, which are college endow-ments, wealthy individuals, and pension funds.

Venture capitalists enjoy the luxury of being able to play a Las Vegas game of odds. They can spread their private investments over twenty or twenty-five companies in a rela-tively short period of time. If a handful of their investments fail outright, these venture investors may shed a brief tear, but the reality is they are always betting that just two to three of their portfolio investments will turn out to be the next multi-billion-dollar tech juggernaut.

In the venture capital game, all it takes is one or two Sammy Sosas to emerge from a portfolio to make up for all the strikeout victims they may have invested in. You as an entrepreneur can never play this same high-risk game of averages. Your business's life is quite simple. It will end either in success or failure. It's not even three strikes and you're out for an entrepreneur. It's one strike and game over! So under-stand from the beginning that the rules of the game are quite different for you than for your potential investment partners and their long-term aspirations for your company.

As an entrepreneur and business owner, you are never like the typical venture capitalist. You are not looking for your company to become either the next instant flameout or giant home run. You would like at the very least to feed your family and pay your bills for a few years, even if your busi-ness is barely limping along. Not surprisingly, as Art Technology founder Jeet Singh points out, a moderately successful company is largely a waste of time for venture capitalists. Zombie companies suck out the moneymen's precious time and resources while offering only a mediocre financial return.

The first step an entrepreneur must consider in the money-raising process is to decide if venture capital is indeed the right move for your company. Once you're in, there's no turning back! Only if you're truly ready for your business to turn into a huge success or absolutely nothing at all should you even consider venture capital. As an entrepreneur or startup executive, you will be entering a high stakes game that will end either in a multi-million-dollar mansion or a cardboard box under the highway overpass. Okay, so that's a little extreme, but there's rarely any in-between!

JEET SINGH

Founder and Chief Executive Officer of Art Technology Group

Q **Ragas:** There are a number of different myths and preconceptions out there about venture capitalists and the private investment business. What do entrepreneurs and business owners need to understand about this industry?

A **Singh:** I think the most critical and problematic thing for entrepreneurs to understand is when venture capitalists claim they are out to make money just like you. The reality is that the philosophy they use to accomplish this is very much like gambling. Most venture capitalists really don't care if 80 percent of their companies drop off the face of the earth, although some claim that they do. As long as a few of the venture capitalists' investments are home runs, they will enjoy astonishing success. But if you're a business owner, that's not your goal. Your goal isn't to have either a huge hit or a flameout! You'd like to be able to pay your bills. Even if your company is just ticking along, you'd rather be ticking along than dead!

Q **Ragas:** So what you're saying is that venture capitalists are fundamentally playing an entirely different ballgame than the company founder or startup's management team. Venture capitalists can play the percentages and roll the dice with their portfolio of investments, whereas the startup and the entrepreneur only have one chance to succeed or fail.

A **Singh:** Right. That's what's kind of odd about venture capital, and it's what most people don't understand. Be careful to find out what the venture capitalists want you to achieve, because typically they make you shoot for a huge win or nothing at all! Four out of five times that they shake your hand, your company is probably going to end up dead. They don't care which. As a business owner, that's not your goal. You'd like to be in business, even if you're just barely surviving, a few years from now. Not so venture capitalists. They don't want barely surviving companies in their portfolios. Struggling companies take up too much attention, time, and effort for the venture capitalist.

"Be careful to find out what the venture capitalists want you to achieve, because typically they make you shoot for a huge win or nothing at all!"

Prove Your Business Model First

If you decide that venture capital is right for your business, then the next step in the capital-raising process is to begin building your company. Give it real legs. Take your whiteboard sketches and take them into the trenches with you. Even though it may feel like a sizeable accomplishment, developing a great idea into a working business model is just the initial foundation for your company. A sturdy foundation by itself is nice but means very little in the grand scheme of things. An entrepreneur has to build actual walls and a roof on top of his business model before he can begin speaking with venture capitalists.

I can tell you that nothing turns off a venture capitalist quicker than an entrepreneur looking to raise capital for an idea that is still a paper tiger. Savvy venture capitalists can see right through a startup that looks like a ferocious tiger on the outside but when it opens its mouth is toothless and has no claws on its paws. Prove your business concept first. Until you can walk into a venture capitalist's office, look him right in the eye, and say, "I know my business works," then you're wasting everyone's time. Think about it. If you're not 100 percent confident that your business concept actually works, why would strangers with a big checkbook feel any different? Trust me, they won't.

Not only does proving your business model first give you more confidence, it will also significantly enhance your bargaining power when you go looking to raise venture capital. More important, it will force your company to run itself like a startup should—lean and mean—with a focus on controlling costs and the bottom line. Far too many startups have been funded without showing a proof of concept first. As Dave Goldberg of Launch Media advises, there is a real advantage to a company proving its business model before accepting venture capital.

Venture capitalists will never point out that suddenly receiving millions of dollars in capital can be very distracting to a startup's management team. Receiving too much money too early usually breeds bad habits that may prove fatal to your business. I've seen venture-backed companies that became bloated so quickly with capital that they lost all sight of their initial goals. For your own protection, take your business model for a test drive first before you start pounding the pavement for capital. Make sure that the wheels don't fall off and that the engine runs smoothly, because once you enter the Indy 500, there's no turning back. Your life will start passing before your eyes faster than you can imagine.

DAVID GOLDBERG

Founder, Chief Executive Officer, and Chairman of Launch Media

Q **Ragas:** You were forced to self-fund your business in the early days entirely with credit card debt and sheer chutzpah. So what advice do you have for entrepreneurs who are eager to go out and raise a monster round of venture capital as soon as they come up with what they think is a hot new idea?

A **Goldberg:** Unfortunately, there is just no simple way to learn. You can't go to school to learn venture capital. You can't have someone just tell you about it, either. The only real way to learn how to do it is to actually do it. That being said, I do think that if you've got a really good business and a management team that executes, then you can raise money even in a difficult environment. We raised money in a very difficult environment to launch what was at the time an unproven online media company. We literally had people laugh out loud at us! Venture capitalist Tim Draper of Draper Fisher Jurvetson just laughed at us. He thought we had a good idea but that we would never be able to pull it off. It's sort of fun to go back to Tim Draper and prove him wrong.

Q **Ragas:** So entrepreneurs must first understand that the best way to learn about the private capital business is to actually go through the process. Before that, though, entrepreneurs can prepare themselves for the process by having a good business model and a management team in place, right?

A **Goldberg:** Yes. Admittedly, we were two guys with absolutely no experience. In the very beginning everybody was looking at the Internet as a software business, and everyone said you're not software guys. So I think the dynamics of who can successfully start tech companies has changed over time. You can never give up. Not having a lot of money forces your

> *"Not having a lot of money forces your company to decide what's critical and what's not critical."*

company to decide what's critical and what's not critical. It forces you to build a culture that thinks of itself as a raw startup at all times. I see a lot of these other start-ups wasting money on so many little things. While I'd have liked our company to have grown a bit faster than it did, we sort of think of ourselves as the tortoise. We've outlasted a lot of people that had more hype, more money, and all sorts of advantages, because we've focused on building our business and not letting ourselves get distracted.

Venture Capitalists Are in the Business of Making Money

Now I realize that I just spent the last section explaining how important it is to have a proof of concept before knocking on a venture capitalist's door. Yet just having this nifty proof of concept isn't going to make venture capitalists bow down and kiss your feet. Not unless you're some incredibly successful serial entrepreneur like Jim Clark of Netscape, WebMD, and Silicon Graphics fame. An entrepreneur must first understand what really drives these modern day masters of the universe.

Get out of your head this whole feel-good notion that venture capitalists are out there primarily to help nurture and grow fledgling young companies and create wonderful new jobs. That's nice and may be the case for some, but venture capitalists are, first and foremost, wealth creators. Plain and simple. They are in the business of making money and creating wealth—the faster, the better. If they were in the charity business, they'd all be running the United Way, and last time I checked, this wasn't the case! So when pitching moneymen, an entrepreneur must first learn to speak their language: the all-American language of dollars and cents.

Right off the bat, you should be prepared to explain to venture capitalists what kind of return on investment they can expect by investing in your company. This is not always an easy number to come up with, and it does require a certain amount of guesstimating by the entrepreneur. However, you must be willing to step to the plate and give the venture capitalist a firm answer to this question. If you aren't, chances are you still lack some level of confidence in your own business.

The advice of iPrint founder Royal Farros is to always put yourself into the venture capitalists' shoes and not look at investment companies in a negative light, just because they are doing their job. If you were one of them, wouldn't you have the same questions? Of course you would. As much as you may be proud of your business model and core technology, the venture capitalist has to have one eye on the future as he tries to figure out what kind of investment return appears feasible from your company. Use this knowledge as an advantage over the thousands of other entrepreneurs jockeying for the same venture capitalist's attention, and you will be one quantum leap ahead of the competition.

ROYAL P. FARROS

Chairman, Founder,
and Chief Executive Officer of iPrint, Inc.

Q **Ragas:** Do you have any particular advice and guidelines for what entrepreneurs and executives at startups must accomplish to capture the attention and interests of tier-one venture capitalists?

A **Farros:** Writing a really great executive summary and an existing proof of concept is very important. I've always found that if you can look venture capital people in the eye and tell them that you already know your business works, then they're going to be a lot more in tune to it! The biggest tip that I can give entrepreneurs is to understand what venture capitalists really want to know. They don't want to get into understanding your company's core technology. What they want to understand right away is how much money they can make by investing in your company! I don't

> *"What they want to understand right away is how much money they can make by investing in your company!"*

mean to say that in a negative way, but venture people are in the business of making money. So whenever venture capitalists look at an idea, there are three or four things they always want to know. Some of these questions are: How big is the market you are going after? Is this the team that can actually make this product or service come to life in that market? If this is the right team for the new idea, what kind of competition are you going to face? Finally, a venture investment decision always comes down to this question: What kind of return on investment can the venture capitalist expect to make by investing in your company? That's the most important question of all!

Target Top-Tier Venture Capitalists

Once you understand the mentality of venture capitalists and what motivates them, the next step is to begin researching which venture capital firms would be the ideal investors in your company. The past decade has marked the emergence of a number of specialized venture capital firms that focus on specific sectors in the technology universe. Very few private capital firms today are still generalists willing to consider almost any investment opportunity, regardless of the sector or stage of the deal. Rather, most firms today focus on specific sectors, such as software, wireless, interactive media, and Internet infrastructure, as well as the actual investment round—ranging from seed stage to mezzanine—that the venture firm usually participates in.

Some first-time entrepreneurs end up mailing off business plans and wasting valuable introductions to venture firms that don't even remotely invest in the sector of the entrepreneur's business. Don't make this costly mistake. Invest real time. Approach the correct venture capitalists. When I say research, I'm not talking about just surfing the Web and reading a bunch of Web sites of venture capital firms.

Leverage your existing network of business contacts. Speak to lawyers, accountants, and other professionals about the venture capitalists they would recommend. Finally, seek out venture-backed entrepreneurs in your area. These entrepreneurs are by far the most valuable sources of advice on venture capital firms that may fit with your business opportunity.

Unfortunately, few entrepreneurs seem to understand that all venture capitalists are not created equal. Like any other profession, the difference between the top tier and the middle of the pack in venture capital land is immense, as Chris MacAskill of MightyWords.com will explain. Go after the cream of the crop. Don't jump on the first venture investor who calls out of the blue and starts waving dollar bills under your nose. Just as you wouldn't trust a life-threatening operation to a doctor who just received his medical degree, you should not be careless about selecting your venture capital partners. Be cautious, be meticulous.

Get references. Start at the top and go after venture capitalists who have already taken companies to the Promised Land. A premier venture capitalist will be able to open doors to potential investment banking, media, and industry relationships that a run-of-the-mill investor can just dream about!

Once a venture capitalist has invested in your company, the experience will feel a lot like a stranger has suddenly moved into your house and is involved in almost every domestic dispute. Do your homework. Pick a venture partner that you actually want walking around your house in slippers and a bathrobe each morning. Choose wisely, because a sub-par venture capitalist is a lot like the crazy uncle who moves in and never leaves!

CHRIS MACASKILL

Founder and Chairman of FatBrain.com;
Chief Executive Officer of MightyWords.com

Q **Ragas:** There is a lot of debate among entrepreneurs about the differences between venture capital firms and the values they all bring to the table. So what have you found is important for entrepreneurs to look for when they decide to head down the venture capital path?

A **MacAskill:** First and foremost, entrepreneurs must realize that venture capitalists are just like any other professionals, such as lawyers or photographers. The top venture capitalists are really, really good and far better than the tier B and tier C ones. As a start-up company, you should always go for the absolute best you can get! There are a lot of vulture capitalists in this world and clueless private investors that companies should flatly avoid. It's not easy to be an amazing venture capitalist like John Doerr of Kleiner Perkins or Bob Kagle of Benchmark Capital. These guys hit balls out of the park all of the time. They've done it time after time! These are the venture capitalists who really know what they're doing.

Q **Ragas:** In other words, picking a venture capitalist is a lot like picking a good doctor. If someone is about to undergo life-threatening surgery, they are most likely going to go with the doctor with a proven record of success. Entrepreneurs should act the same way when they go about selecting an investment partner.

A **MacAskill:** Yes. Someone like John Doerr builds companies to last. In fact, he still sits on the board of Sun Microsystems. The first thing an entrepreneur must do is go after the top-tier venture capitalists as potential investors. Now, following my own rule, I actually stiffed a venture capitalist who had just formed a new fund and wasn't that well-known yet. It turned out to be a terrible mistake. It was Bob Kagle, one of the founders of Benchmark Capital. I would have been one of his first investments! I turned him down. I'll have to live that one down somehow.

"First and foremost, entrepreneurs must realize that venture capitalists are just like any other professionals."

Use Your Contacts to Get an Introduction

After you've put together a short list of venture capitalists you feel could be a good match for your business, it is time to start making contact with these select moneymen. Here's where things can start to get tricky. Placing dozens of phone calls, showing up in these firms' lobbies, and even mailing them beautifully crafted business plans on gold parchment is not going to get you anywhere. Shooting up flares and sending smoke signals isn't going to work either. I don't care if you have a team of dancing chorus girls show up at a venture capitalist's office to personally deliver your plan. No one's going to look at it.

Venture capitalists only do deals that originate within their existing network of contacts. Unless you can get a friend of a venture capitalist to personally drop off your plan or executive summary, chances are that ninety-nine times out of a hundred, your business plan is going straight into the wastebasket. I know that might seem harsh, but it's the truth. Without a proper introduction into the venture capital labyrinth, "cold," unsolicited business plans just get old and grow mold. Unless you're trying out some bizarre new science experiment, this is definitely not the result you are looking for!

The key to breaking into the inner circle of venture capital is to use your own network of business and social contacts. Utilize lawyers, accountants, and executives at venture-backed companies whom you already know and trust to give you introductions into the venture capital firms on your list. Many of these people know the hidden handshakes and secret oaths of venture capital society and are in a position to say a good word for you. Venture capitalists are willing at least to hear a quick pitch or skim an executive summary that hits their desk from one of these sources.

Sit down and make up a list of your professional contacts. Take your time. Be thorough. Entrepreneurs are usually surprised at how many people they know and the number of contacts they can come up with. As an entrepreneur, this is an extremely trying part of the process and takes incredible persistence and stamina.

As Sportsline.com founder Mike Levy points out, he was flatly turned down twice by Kleiner Perkins before he found the proper introduction into this venture capital power-house. Kleiner eventually became a sizeable Sportsline investor. Never underestimate the power of a well-placed and credible introduction into the venture capital kingdom. The future of your startup may depend on it.

MICHAEL LEVY

Founder, Chairman, and
Chief Executive Office of CBS Sportsline.com

Q **Ragas:** There are a lot of different myths and misconceptions about successfully breaking into the venture capital labyrinth.

What are some tricks of the trade that you've learned over the course of your career?

A **Levy:** The most important thing is to be introduced properly to a venture capitalist. One of the mistaken notions among many entrepreneurs is that a business plan sent through the mail to a venture capitalist will actually be read! After venture capital firm Kleiner Perkins funded us, I talked to one of the firm's partners who was on our board of directors about this. He said that he doesn't know of any venture capitalist who's ever invested in a company after receiving an unsolicited business plan, because venture capitalists just don't have time to read all the material they receive. Venture capitalists are all busy as hell. Among other things, they're sitting on a bunch of different boards of companies they've funded. To save time, they only look at business plans brought to them by individuals they know and trust. Kleiner Perkins funded my company because I went in to Netscape and met with former Netscape president Jim Barksdale and a bunch of key executives there. Netscape really liked the concept, Kleiner Perkins had already invested in Netscape, and so Netscape walked me in the door at Kleiner Perkins. That was the first time I was taken seriously. Kleiner Perkins had already turned me down twice before then. The right introduction is the key.

> *"One of the mistaken notions among many entrepreneurs is that a business plan sent through the mail to a venture capitalist will actually be read!"*

Convince Investors You Are a Viable Market Opportunity

Let's continue under the scenario that a few well-placed introductions have succeeded in landing your company face-to-face meetings with a few venture capitalists on your wish list. First, give yourself a small pat on the back. Few entrepreneurs ever get the opportunity to step inside the hallowed offices of these kings of capitalism. Fewer still are able to say they were invited back for a second meeting or actually walked away with a deal in hand. Maybe you will be one of the select few to accomplish this lofty feat. Having read this book, you will go to the first meeting knowing how venture capitalists think and what they want to hear, and that is more than half the battle.

Your goal should be to convince your potential investor that there is a viable market opportunity surrounding your fledgling business. Don't waste time at the first meeting explaining your nifty new technology, exciting management team, and how you're going to crush the competition. None of these will matter if you aren't able to convince the venture capitalist that here is a sizeable and uncluttered market opportunity. Venture investors have little patience. Pretend that you are speaking to a bunch of hyperactive children who haven't had their Ritalin for the day. Be quick and succinct. Grab their attention.

If you succeed, you'll more than likely find yourself barraged with a number of tough questions and a hearty scoop of skepticism and disbelief. Be prepared to defend the many investment risks that your inquisitors will undoubtedly toss in your direction. These risks can range from questions about the depth and talent level of your management team, the threat from existing competition in the marketplace, and the soundness of your company's technology. Whatever the case, your job is to minimize these apparent risks in the investors' minds.

It doesn't matter if you agree with these apparent risks or not. Defend them, minimize them, and clearly explain to the venture capitalist how you plan to eliminate them. If you haven't got such a plan or choose not to listen to the investors' objections, then you are asking for a quick nail in your company's coffin. Don't let this happen. As Ventro's David Perry explains, the second job of an entrepreneur in any capital-raising meeting is to answer the potential venture capitalists' objections and convince them that the risks are manageable. If you can achieve this goal, you are within striking distance of receiving an investment term sheet. You've thrown your bait in the water, and you have a big fish biting. Now take your time reeling him in.

DAVID PERRY

President and Chief Executive Officer of Ventro

Q **Ragas:** Let's assume that an entrepreneur has successfully attracted the interest of a handful of venture capital firms. What guidelines and ground rules do you have for entrepreneurs and executives who are only a few steps away from actually closing a round of venture capital?

A **Perry:** Venture capitalists are pretty simple organisms. They look at the world in a no-nonsense way. The first question a venture capitalist asks will be geared to understanding if there is really a market opportunity tied to the idea that the entrepreneur is proposing. If the answer to that question is yes, then in theory the venture capitalist wants to invest at some price. The next question you will be asked relates to risk. What could go wrong? The makeup of your management team, the competitive climate, and technology-related issues are risks that may be mentioned. You really have two jobs here. One is to convince the venture capitalist that you represent an opportunity. That's usually a big hurdle to clear! If you can do that, you're halfway there. The second job of the entrepreneur is to convince the venture capitalist that you can minimize the risks of the opportunity or at least that the risks are manageable. Listen carefully to what the venture capitalists think the business risks are. It's less important what you think they are and more important what they think they are! If you can convince them that you can minimize these risks and at some price, they will invest.

Q **Ragas:** Entrepreneurs must not only convince venture capitalists that they represent a real investment opportunity, but they also must work hard to minimize the potential risks the venture capitalist has uncovered. If the risks aren't addressed, your company may have trouble securing additional financing down the line.

A **Perry:** Right. The entrepreneur's entire job after raising the first round of venture capital is to minimize or get rid of the risks, so that when you need to come back and raise additional capital you can just repeat the process. In raising the next round of capital, entrepreneurs should follow the process I described for the first round, except that they should explain to the venture capitalists that the opportunity has become even larger than it was before! If you do your job, the venture capitalists will see the same opportunity with less risk surrounding it. They will then be willing to invest even more money in your business and at an even higher valuation!

"The first question a venture capitalist asks will be geared to understanding if there is really a market opportunity tied to the idea that the entrepreneur is proposing."

It's Term Sheet Time!

Once you've managed to prove that you are pursuing a real market opportunity and can minimize or even eliminate the investment risks, the chances are that your investors will be ready to talk valuation. The game will begin with each side suggesting how much this business idea and existing startup is really worth. Unless your company appears poised to became the next JDS Uniphase or Netscape, the venture capitalist is going to automatically have the upper hand in these discussions. Fortunately, there are a variety of ways to level the playing field. First of all, an entrepreneur or startup executive should hire an experienced venture capital attorney for all stages of this negotiation. Having an experienced entrepreneur or business executive who has been through this process before to rely on as counsel can also be invaluable. If your company does appear to be uniquely hot and sought after in the marketplace, there is the chance that you will receive a number of offers from various investment firms. When played off one against another strategically, this rabid interest can shoot up the valuation of your company almost overnight. However, this same strategy can backfire miserably if any of the potential investors feel that they are being used.

The incredible boom in venture capital over the past few years has numbed many entrepreneurs to the traditional rigors and challenges of the fund-raising process. Even with the recent vicious shakeout among many private Internet companies, too many entrepreneurs still expect venture capitalists to come chasing after them instead of the other way around. One mental hurdle private companies must overcome when they accept venture capital is the reality that they will more than likely have to sell a sizeable minority stake in their fledgling startup. In addition, you're more than likely going to think your company is worth more than the price your investor is willing to pay. This is okay. It's part of the game. Learn to accept it, or don't head down the venture capital route at all.

If you really believe in the long-term prospects of your business, selling a portion to obtain the much-needed capital rocket fuel to further grow your idea should be a welcome experience. Never forget that the right venture capitalists can dramatically enhance the value of your company, virtually overnight. Learn to understand and appreciate the concept of "big pie–small piece." John Holt, the founder of the Cobalt Group, did. If he hadn't, there is no telling what his company would look like today, or if it would still exist. Remember, owning a hundred percent of something worth zero is still zero, no matter how many ways you slice it. On the other hand, owning a healthy slice of a pie that has grown big enough to feed a continent is another story. Keep this in mind at term sheet time. Unless you quickly get over the fears of ownership dilution, you'll eternally be driving your company with one foot firmly on the brake!

JOHN HOLT

Chief Executive Officer and Founder of The Cobalt Group

Q **Ragas:** The past few years have seen venture capital flowing more freely than ever before into technology companies. What lessons do you have for entrepreneurs who are weighing investment offers from various venture capital firms?

A **Holt:** There's a famous story in the Seattle high-tech community about how many people the well-known entrepreneur Paul Brainard had to call on to raise money in the early days of Aldus Computers. I don't know the exact number of people Brainard called, but I heard it was more than 180 venture firms. That may sound like a lot, but we actually called on more people than that just to get Cobalt initially funded! The lesson here is that you really have to be willing to talk to at least a few hundred different people if you are really serious about getting investment capital for your company. You have to be prepared to sell your idea to the investment community. You've got to be willing to talk to almost anyone who will listen. It's almost a test of the passion. By the time we finally raised money, we were running on fumes and had literally been borrowing from credit cards to cover payroll!

Q **Ragas:** So what you're saying is that successfully raising money from venture capitalists is a long, drawn-out process that often comes down to tenacity and persistence. In your case, you were literally bootstrapping your business for years, but never gave up.

A **Holt:** Yes, we totally bootstrapped the business in the early days. When a deal finally came along, we had no other bids for our stock from other venture capitalists. First Analysis was the only venture capital company that was interested, and we knew that the only deal we had was the best deal we had! We accepted the investment from them in return for a 50 percent ownership stake in our company. I really didn't feel that we were being taken advantage of! First Analysis drove a hard bargain, but it wasn't a punitive bargain. Although we gave up half the company, we knew we were doing the right thing. Entrepreneurs must quickly get used to the concept of "big pie–small piece" when dealing with venture capitalists. That was a philosophy we adopted early on. Even today, I don't get too hung up about stock ownership dilution. It's not that I don't care about dilution, but we have never put the company at risk by walking away from a deal. Entrepreneurs should always be more focused on long-term opportunity than the size of their piece of the pie.

> *"Entrepreneurs must quickly get used to the concept of "big pie–small piece" when dealing with venture capitalists."*

What About High-Net-Worth Individuals?

As much as venture capitalists might not like to admit it, these mystical moneymen are not the only people who hold the keys to the venture capital kingdom. The tech boom of the past decade has produced a number of successful technology entrepreneurs who now have access to significant personal capital. Many of them are very sophisticated investors eager to back promising startups. While high-net-worth individuals used to be active only in a company's seed stage funding, they are increasingly moving up the food chain and investing in later rounds of financing as well.

In fact, there are now a handful of high-profile examples, most notably PurchasePro.com, Embarcadero Technologies, and InfoSpace, of companies that made it all the way to the public markets without ever accepting any form of traditional venture capital. Instead, all of these companies were backed by groups of high-net-worth individuals. The obvious upside to dealing with these angel investors is that they typically have more time to roll up their sleeves and work with an entrepreneur than a busy venture capitalist might have. As PurchasePro.com chief Junior Johnson notes, private investors also typically show more patience in waiting for their investments to blossom. At the same time, though, it is important to note that there are also clear downsides to raising capital from high-net-worth individuals.

I strongly urge companies to only target high-net-worth investors whose backgrounds line up well with your core focus area. Otherwise, you run the risk of being associated with a group of investors that add little real value beyond their capital. To make matters worse, no one really likes to deal with a company backed by "dumb money." Since capital is merely a commodity today, tapping into a financial backer's network of contacts and expertise is often where the real value lies for your company's future.

For this reason, most entrepreneurs would be best served in later rounds of financing to raise capital from traditional venture capital sources. The best "venture capital gumbo" today is a mixture of high-net-worth individuals with expertise in your focus area, and established venture capital firms. Now, get to work on assembling these ingredients!

CHARLES JOHNSON JR.

Founder, Chairman, and
Chief Executive Officer of PurchasePro.com

Q **Ragas:** The current technology boom has placed us in an environment where almost every entrepreneur is eager to rush out and raise venture capital. What advice do you have for entrepreneurs who are considering the institutional venture capital route for their businesses?

A **Johnson:** The first key is to avoid venture capital if at all possible, because it is very "expensive." As an entrepreneur, you've worked your guts out developing the technology and building the business. Then at the eleventh hour a venture capitalist slides in and takes a significant piece of the equity in your business. This person is generally just an opportunist. He who controls the money controls the deal. In other words, line up your money before you do the deal. Entrepreneurs often have the mistaken impression that once you've got a good deal everyone is going to come running to invest. Well, if you've got the money behind the deal before you even get started, then you can control the deal throughout! As an entrepreneur, you may find you spend more time raising money than running the business. High-net-worth people are often the best source of capital, because most of them have somewhere in their business lives already embarked upon a similar journey, or they wouldn't be high-net-worth!

Q **Ragas:** Right. High-net-worth individuals are mostly all former entrepreneurs themselves who understand many of the challenges that must be overcome in growing a business from scratch. They've already personally encountered during their own careers many of the same mountains that must be climbed by the new entrepreneur.

A **Johnson:** Yes. High-net-worth individuals understand that there are going to be ups and downs to your business. They don't have unrealistic expectations. That's not so with lots of venture capitalists today who are young, get-rich-quick kind of people who are opportunists. There was a time a few years ago when these people were important, but today entrepreneurs have the ability to raise money through high-net-worth people instead. I think it's a much more valuable opportunity. Angel investors aren't trying to bat five out of ten or seven out of ten like many venture capitalists. High-net-worth individuals are trying to bat ten out of ten! You're going to get more patience and people who actually understand the business. You are going to receive much more constructive advice and longer-term support if you decide to turn to high-net-worth individuals.

> *"High-net-worth people are often the best source of capital, because most of them have somewhere in their business lives already embarked upon a similar journey, or they wouldn't be high-net-worth!"*

CHAPTER 4

MARKETING AND SALES STRATEGIES THAT WORK

THE GIGANTIC SEQUOIA TREES ARE AMONG THE WORLD'S GREAT natural wonders. Growing to more than 300 feet tall and 20 feet across, these trees, each the size of the Statue of Liberty and the largest on earth, have lived for almost 3,000 years. Anyone who has ever visited a giant Sequoia grove in the Sierra Nevada mountains of Central California knows the absolute beauty, suffocating power, and mind-numbing size of these trees. I think these gigantic trees are the perfect images for today's cluttered market, filled with entrenched competitors that fledgling young technology startups must overcome with the right mix of sales and marketing.

Just like a tired hiker lost among the giant Sequoias, a fledgling tech company can find it extremely difficult to be noticed among the looming giants of the marketplace—no matter how much the company founders wave their arms and jump. In this situation it is easy for the company to become frustrated trying to find its target customers. All too often, these companies fall into a vicious downward spiral of wasted marketing dollars and sales experiments gone terribly wrong. To correct their mistakes, these startups resort to equally misguided tactics like $2 million Super Bowl ads and lavish "launch" parties fit for the Queen of England. Fortunately, it doesn't have to be this way.

There are real ways to rise above the Goliaths of the marketplace and to cost effectively establish and maintain meaningful and long-lasting customer relationships. As I'll show you in this chapter, companies should not open their new lemonade stands in the middle of a Sequoia grove in the first place. After all, that's exactly where existing companies hope that startups will decide to begin—in the middle of the crowded forest they already own. In fact, "legacy" companies are more like the gigantic trees than any of us imagine. Sequoias, with their unusually thick, fire-resistant bark, depend on periodic fires to wipe out the firs and pines that would otherwise take over the forest. This sounds a lot like the periodic market corrections of the technology industry that have regularly wiped out waves of new startups, while leaving older technology organizations largely intact. New companies that survive these corrections usually have found the right mix of marketing and sales savvy. They endure and continue to grow while companies with the wrong mix fail.

The right mix is crucial. With the wrong mix, marketing and sales can be an eternal black hole in your organization that you must keep feeding each month. However, with proper nourishment and support, your sales and marketing team should be able to grow and thrive on its own. A smart company provides its sales force with the marketing tools and operating environment needed to feed itself. The days of throwing sales and marketing dollars against a wall and seeing what sticks are long gone. Capital is no longer free. Generating a consistent return on investment in the sales and marketing realm has become paramount.

As I'll show you in this chapter, by applying the right blend of digital fertilizers and other important nutrients, companies can grow with the giants in the marketplace and cost effectively acquire and retain their target customers. We will first explore ways to lower the cost of deployment for a product or service, with Net Perceptions founder Steven Snyder. Tumbleweed chief Jeff Smith will then share with us the benefits of immediately establishing a direct sales force. Building these direct relationships is key for turning your early clients into marketing evangelists for your company, as Speechworks CEO Stu Patterson will explain.

Next, I will share with you the benefits of focusing on lead generation and measurable results when it comes time to shell out big bucks on advertising and marketing. As Digex founder Doug Humphrey notes, it is little coincidence that companies often do their most effective marketing when they are cash-strapped startups. We will then look at what kinds of digital advertising do and don't work online, with the help of Web veteran and CitySearch founder Charles Conn. Finally, this section will detail the importance of understanding that the sales and marketing process in a technology organization is like a track runner who never takes a water break. High-tech sales and marketing simply never rests or sleeps, as BroadVision CEO Pehong Chen reminds us. In other words, if it moves—sell to it!

Do Whatever It Takes to Lower Deployment Costs

The first step in devising a successful digital marketing and sales strategy should actually begin before the final version of your new product rolls off the assembly line or your new service is offered to the outside world. Closely inspect your new product or service and understand how it will be used by your potential customer. Kick the tires a little and give it a good test run—not in an R&D lab, but out in the field where it belongs. Then take it out of the hands of your engineering and operations team and put it into the arms of the sales and marketing cowboys. These are the troops that must now become strident believers in your new product or service.

Let them manhandle and abuse your new toy. Then listen carefully to this group's feedback, praise, and even disgust. You can rest assured you will receive quite candid feedback from your sales force, since their livelihood depends directly on the soundness of this new product or service. They know if it doesn't sell well, they'll be buying meals at McDonald's rather than at five-star restaurants. Value their criticism and act on it. More than likely after this criticism, your product or service will still be more complex, more difficult, and more expensive to market and sell than you had originally anticipated. This is no good. In fact, it reeks of impending failure. Save yourself future pain and suffering. Go back and remove any mention of more complex and more difficult from your vocabulary. Become a master of simplicity. Always build solutions for a group of hyperactive adolescents—not rocket scientists with too much time on their hands. Your new solution must immediately scream, "I'm simple" to have any chance of being accepted in the marketplace. Think simple, be simple, and create simple solutions. Simple sells. I'm dead serious. We live in a society of microwave meals, drive-up ATMs, and real-time stock trading. If we had the technology, we would love to beam ourselves around from place to place ala *Star Trek*.

Time is more than money. Time is the judge, jury, and executioner for your new product or service. Simplicity is time's best friend. Throw patience right out the window. If we ever had any patience to begin with, it's now long gone. Which means that lowering the cost of deployment for your new product or service has become the first major hurdle that your company must overcome in launching a successful sales and marketing strategy. This cost of deployment ultimately falls into two categories: additional capital expenditures and time constraints. Think of every product or service as having a cost-benefit curve. The more you can ride down the cost of deployment, the more net benefits you will provide your customer.

Suppose Microsoft went off the deep end tomorrow and decided that its new edition of Microsoft Office would only work on Cray supercomputers, not desktop computers. The company would effectively be increasing the cost of deployment and adoption for its software. This is an extreme example, but many companies develop solutions without seriously keeping in mind the related products and services that the consumer must upgrade or purchase beforehand to properly utilize this new solution. The failure of high-profile, band-width-intensive online entertainment companies like POP.com, Pseudo, and DEN are largely due to cost of deployment issues. All three of these companies underestimated the limited roll-out to date of widespread broadband technology needed to enjoy these sites. Low bandwidth gaming sites like Gamesville and Uproar continue to thrive, since they are available to anyone on the Internet regardless of Net connection speeds.

Also doomed on arrival are new products and services that suck down minutes—even seconds—of precious time by a customer and come with a significant learning curve to install or properly deploy. Think about this for a second. What would happen to the auto industry if new cars came shipped in a big box all in pieces and, worse yet, your new car needs a specific brand of gasoline or it will not run? Thankfully, I don't think we'll ever have to worry about this happening, but this is exactly why many new technology-focused products and services fail. They eat away at time and precious resources instead of seamlessly integrating into the environment of the customer right away.

Don't let the cost of deployment drag your new product or service down into the muck and mire with other solutions of questionable value propositions. As Net Perceptions founder and former Microsoft executive Steven Snyder points out, simple sells, while complex just makes customers yell. So find ways to turn the cost-benefit curve into your best friend, and you will have given your sales and marketing team a huge shot in the arm!

STEVEN SNYDER

Cofounder and Chairman of Net Perceptions

Q **Ragas:** One of the first steps that technology companies must take to enjoy real sales and marketing success is to develop a product or service that really creates unique value for the customer. What other advice do you have for companies looking to improve their sales and marketing process?

A **Snyder:** The most important objective to achieve is to demonstrate customer value. Your company must be able to actually go in and deploy your solution or sell your product and immediately show that it adds value and that it works. That is a very important art to learn. It really comes down to understanding your customer's needs and making sure that your product fits the needs of the market that you are trying to serve. Ease of deployment, next to actually demonstrating that your solution adds value, is the most important thing. Basically, there is a cost-benefit curve for any product or service. The more your company can bring down the cost of deployment, the more net benefits you are going to add to your customer. You can ride down cost of deployment through things like partnerships that help reduce complexity and costs. A company should also make its product or service fit easily and gracefully into the environment of the end-customer. Riding down this cost to deploy curve is very important.

Q **Ragas:** What you're saying, then, is that a company can develop the best mousetrap on the planet, but if that solution is cumbersome and costly for a customer to actually deploy or utilize, then all the sales and marketing in the world won't help you.

A **Snyder:** For every single wave of new technology, the cost of deployment has been one of the fundamental obstacles. I remember an incredibly astute talk that venture capitalist Bill Gurley from Benchmark Capital gave back in 1996 at a conference. He said that backhoes don't obey Moore's Law. This speaks directly to the cost of deployment. What he is saying is that Moore's Law—which is basically that the computational power available at a particular price doubles every eighteen months—is not the "gating" factor for many of the Net infrastructure-focused companies. They are more constrained in their growth by physical factors. He drew a chart of the average price of a Caterpillar tractor and showed how it has not decreased much in price, compared to

"People who are developing products or services need to think about how complicated they are to actually implement and use."

how semiconductors have decreased in price over the years. His point is that there are gating factors in the physical world that don't obey the laws that are relevant to the actual cost of microprocessors. As you probably know, I worked at Microsoft in the eighties, and even though Bill Gates is not known for software that is easy to use, his mantra was that software always should be simple. He pounded this into everyone's mind. People who are developing products or services need to think about how complicated they are to actually implement and use.

Think Direct, Be Direct, Interact

Once you have lowered the cost of the deployment side of the cost-benefit curve for your new product or service, it is time to strengthen the customer interaction side of the sales and marketing process. You may be tempted to run out and throw marketing dollars at a traditional advertising campaign, but you will be more richly rewarded if you first spend the time to build a direct sales force from the ground up. I realize that the concept of building a direct sales team goes against the fanciful myth of the virtual corporation that does almost all of its sales through nifty alliances and partnerships. While this may be the case for companies with ironclad proprietary technologies, the rest of the digital world has succeeded by rolling up its sleeves and getting out directly into the field.

When a company is first starting out, the direct sales force is the only group of people who really care if the product or service fails or succeeds. Feel-good alliances with existing complementary companies don't really matter until you establish a core demand in the market for your product or service. Don't put yourself in the unfortunate position of being the fairy-tale deal of the day. Building a direct sales arm of your organization will allow you to gain early traction in the market and will also provide you with direct feedback from early customers. When this feedback is mined properly, it can allow your company to tweak your product or service to meet market needs in a way that companies that rely on other sales channels can't do nearly as fast.

That's what makes the direct sales model so incredibly lethal. Not only does it allow for much greater efficiency in the supply chain, it also places companies in constant direct contact with their customers. In a world that is constantly changing, being able to meet the evolving needs of a customer day in and day out puts your company in a class far above organizations still stuck using other companies and retailers as their primary interface with customers. You don't want to erect these "walls" between your customer and your sales force. This is not to say that partnerships and alliances don't have their place in every successful digital-focused business today. However, it is only after a company's product or service has learned how to fly on its own that it typically begins to generate a significant percentage of sales.

Even leading software and new media companies like Oracle, Sun Microsystems, Yahoo, and America Online rely primarily on their own sales forces for staying intimately aware of changing customer needs and demand in the marketplace. As Tumbleweed founder and CEO Jeff Smith explains, a company must constantly breathe in the many varied needs of its customers if it hopes to survive. If this relationship with the customer becomes cluttered or blocked by third parties, the chances are high that the company will eventually suffocate and die. So bring an oxygen tank to the battle. Build a direct sales and marketing operation as soon as possible.

JEFFREY SMITH

Founder, Chief Executive Officer,
and President of Tumbleweed Communications

Q **Ragas:** Startups, as well as many offline companies, are struggling today to find ways to slice through all the "noise" in the marketplace to reach their customers. What is the key to the sales and marketing process for digital businesses?

A **Smith:** There are two types of companies in the technology world. There are companies that are good at marketing and there are companies that are good at selling. America Online and eBay are companies that are good at marketing. Ariba and Oracle are companies that are good at selling. Tumbleweed is a company that's also good at selling. One way of cracking the code and getting real traction with products or services is to build a direct sales organization with a services organization right along side it. Companies should speak to a lot of customers and figure out firsthand their problems.

"The fact is that customer interaction helps pin down what the customer really needs and is therefore the air supply a company must breathe to be successful."

This gives companies the flexibility to come back with solutions that meet those customers' requirements. Any company is naïve if it thinks it can be successful with a horizontal solution that supposedly works for everyone. It's just not possible! If you are a marketing or a sales company, you must understand your customers' requirements and put a compelling value proposition on the table that meets those requirements or exceeds them. This is true when you're eBay, but it's also true when you're Tumbleweed. Companies that try to do everything through partnerships will fail. It's not just because the direct road is better than the indirect road. The fact is that customer interaction helps pin down what the customer really needs and is therefore the air supply a company must breathe to be successful. If that air supply is clogged and indirect, you won't get a steady supply of air, and you will eventually fail. Successful companies are the ones that have the tenacity to get in there and are willing to make the investment in sales and marketing to establish direct customer relationships.

Make Your Clients Think You Walk on Water

Once you have a direct sales team firmly in place, you can begin to do what is needed to establish in the customer's mind that you are a special company. When you make promises, you keep them and will do anything to do so. This may seem simple and trite, but keeping promises will pay huge dividends for your business. Customers are so used to being lied to and put off today that organizations that actually follow through on promises are like a breath of fresh air. Think back to the last time you were taken advantage of. It didn't feel good, did it? It stung, and you probably promised yourself that you would never do business with that company again. Learn from your own experience. Don't ever put your company in a situation where it makes promises it can't keep.

If your company can consistently deliver on the promises that it makes, I assure you that you will come to be recognized as a special company in your industry. Regularly under-promise and over-deliver, and you will be truly differentiated from the competition. That's what turns skittish first-time customers into loyal long-term believers. To repeat, delivering on promises is more important than splashy advertising! Once a few key clients become strident believers in your product or service, you will have created the beginning of a sales and marketing tornado that is self-perpetuating. Rest assured, happy customers will tell friends, and friends will tell friends of friends about this "special new company" they have found.

Over time, this reference-ability and powerful word of mouth will become lethal weapons that other firms can't compete against! All of their marketing dollars won't be able to convince a potential customer otherwise. The secret is that people trust the recommendations of friends over the promises they see in a glossy magazine ad or slick television commercial. Ninety-five times out of a hundred, a customer's final decision about a product or service comes down to a reference check of the company's clients. We live in an age where, more than ever before, customers check the reputation of a company and the reliability of a product or service before making a purchase. Internet message board sites and discussion forums featuring quick reviews of every new product and service under the sun are becoming increasingly popular as consumers learn to depend on them.

That's why delivering on promises and being entirely honest and forthright is so crucial for a new company today. The repeat liar is found out and punished faster than in the past. While it has never paid to break promises in business, the always-connected customers of today have the power to turn promise-violators into lepers in almost the blink of an eye. That's why Speechworks CEO Stuart Patterson believes that repeatedly delivering on every promise made to a customer is the quickest and most powerful way to do well in the marketplace today. When your initial customer base comes to the conclusion that your company walks on water, their trust can be leveraged into an infectious group of sales and marketing evangelists for your product or service. Successfully harness word of mouth, and you will have tapped into a marketing asset your competitors cannot quickly imitate.

STUART PATTERSON

President and Chief Executive Officer of Speechworks International

Q **Ragas:** Clearly, a company must first establish, on its own, a demand in the marketplace for its product or service. Then it should look to form partnerships with larger technology organizations. But what other steps can a company take to enhance the sales and marketing side of its organization?

A **Patterson:** One way to rise above the clutter is to deliver on promises. The most powerful marketing tool to rise above the clutter is still word of mouth and customer reference-ability. I remember three years ago when I first joined this company, one of our customers said this was the only company they had done business with in the past few years that actually delivered on every promise it made. From a marketing perspective, if you can find a couple of key accounts that are the top in their fields and make them think you walk on water as a company, you will rise above the clutter quickly, because they will become your best references.

Q **Ragas:** Right. If you can always follow through on your promises and exceed customers' expectations, then existing customers will become your most important sales and marketing asset. In effect, they will become industry champions for your product or service.

A **Patterson:** They will evangelize for you within their organizations and to other organizations. I have always said that everything starts with sales. Engineers may tell you that everything starts with a great product, but I'm not one of the engineers. So I feel that if you can't sell and grow your sales at a certain pace, then ultimately you will fail or flatten out prematurely. If you get into a deal, it will almost always come down to reference checks. You will win out if you always keep your promises. It's not the glitzy advertising that matters, it's the very end of the sales process when you're trying to close the deal. That's when you have to have an asset that your competitors don't have, which is references that think you walk on water.

> *"If you can find a couple of key accounts . . . and make them think you walk on water as a company, you will rise above the clutter quickly, because they will become your best references."*

In Marketing, Less Is Often More

After you have established a direct sales team, as well as built your organization into a company inbred with keeping promises and over-delivering, it becomes time to craft a meaningful marketing message. This is when the marketing department will likely be itching to launch an elaborate advertising campaign and to begin spending your precious capital as if you print money in your basement. Lavish marketing campaigns are fine for companies that have already climbed the mountain of market dominance and are thumping their chests on the top. High-profile campaigns may not be sensible for anyone in my view, but at least big companies can afford them. The first action of many startups after they land a sizeable slug of venture capital is to hire a high-profile Madison Avenue ad agency to quickly whip up an ad campaign.

That is a big mistake. For one thing, in today's crowded technology marketplace, potential customers have become largely immune to force-fed advertising. This is not to say that the occasional television commercial, banner advertisement, or magazine ad doesn't catch the customer's eye, but more often than not a young company's marketing message ends up as a jumbled mess of slogans, pitches, and images in the customer's mind. Second, traditional advertising rarely delivers what a fledgling new company needs the most: new customers! Somewhere in the tech boom of the past decade, many marketers and company executives forgot that the primary purpose of marketing is to generate leads that will eventually turn into long-term customers. While advertising agencies would love you to believe that establishing visibility and an image in the marketplace is just as important, it's not!

While building visibility and creating an image may be just fine and dandy for the ad agency as it gorges itself on lofty placement and creation fees from your company, it's a surefire way to run your company right out of business. It's as if fledgling companies today have forgotten that they're not established heavyweights like Coca-Cola and Pepsi battling for a few percentage points in mature markets where image-based advertising really does matter. Instead, marketing dollars should go directly to generate new sa. Winning fancy advertising industry awards for your brand building ads doesn't really mean anything if you can't pay the bills. As Digex founder and Cidera chief Doug Humphrey points out, marketing is not an end; Marketing is a means to the end. Sales must be the true end goal for any early-stage firm that is ramping up its marketing efforts.

For this reason, I believe that less is often more when creating a successful marketing campaign for a new technology-focused product or service. In my experience, tech companies that initially spend fewer total dollars on marketing usually end up with the best results, because these organizations have forced themselves to think creatively. Instead of spending like a drunken sailor, the company has forced itself to sit down and think through how it can drive sales with a limited budget on the sales and marketing front.

For example, look at free e-mail provider Hotmail, now a Microsoft-owned company. Hotmail ingeniously added the line, "Get your free e-mail at Hotmail," to the end of every outbound e-mail message sent by a Hotmail user. Would they have stumbled on that idea if the company had a sizeable marketing budget? With only a measly $50,000 to spend on marketing, the young company was forced to think out of the box and be different! The end result of this creative marketing tactic is that Hotmail is today by far the largest free e-mail provider on the Web. When the company was purchased by Microsoft in 1998, the price was approximately $400 million in stock!

Many capital-intensive ad campaigns that I see today remind me of a heart surgeon trying to operate on a patient using a chainsaw. Instead of spending time to properly identify their target customers, a lot of companies hack away all over the place and end up looking like a bloody mess. While nate to single out a specific company, failed pet products e-tailer Pets.com is a perfect example of this chainsaw marketing strategy gone terribly awry. The company created some memorable television commercials featuring a lovable sock puppet character, but all they had to show for their efforts was a drained bank account and outrageously high customer-acquisition costs.

Pets.com burned through almost $150 million in capital before deciding to shut its doors. The company's most valuable asset ended up being its well-known sock puppet character. Pets.com's brand name, customer list, and inventory were virtually worthless. I like to think of this as the fable of the $150 million sock puppet spokesman that ended up homeless. If that's not a clear example of how brute marketing force doesn't translate into long-term digital business success, I don't know what is! Whatever you do, learn to paint with a brush, not a roller, when creating your marketing campaign. Remember that less is often more, especially when it forces your company to deliver results.

DOUG HUMPHREY

Founder and Chairman of Cidera; Founder of Digex

Q **Ragas:** We live in a technology world where every company is desperately trying to grab the attention of potential customers. Based on your experience, what would you say is the key to successfully marketing tech products or services?

A **Humphrey:** I'm a big fan of spending less rather than more on marketing. To me, a smaller amount of marketing that has been really thought through works so much better than a large amount of marketing that is just slapped together. Spending tons and tons on marketing is often like using a roller instead of a brush when painting. If you are a consumer brand, it's possible you may get a little more mileage out of the roller and mass-marketing spending. But I've seen a lot of companies with no discipline to their marketing. Many of these companies are very reckless and splash paint all over the place. Companies should never do things just because everyone else is. I think you have to be very wary of that, because a big marketing campaign will make a company burn through their money very fast. I also don't think it gets you anywhere. Marketing is not an end; it's just a means. A sale is an end. Marketing must serve sales by providing lead generation. I've seen a lot of excess spending on advertising recently from companies that are veering away from the basics. They need to think more like guerilla marketers, that is, marketers with a small budget. I don't think it's a coincidence that small, newly capitalized companies with very little money often do the best marketing. Early on is when the company is forced to think hard and be creative. Once companies get a lot of money, too many of them start lathering it all over the place! They forget how to think!

> *"Marketing is not an end; it's just a means. A sale is an end. Marketing must serve sales by providing lead generation."*

Market at the Bottom of the Pyramid

Keeping our mindset of "less is often more" when marketing a new product or service, the next thing to understand is what kind of marketing does and doesn't work in the digital world. As I have already pointed out, I am generally not very keen on most forms of offline marketing (at least initially) for most new products or services. While media like radio, television, newspapers, and magazines all have their place in the marketing of a new solution, these media rarely provide the immediate call to action and trackable results that a fledgling company needs. The marketing of any new product or service must be directly tied to generating leads that end in real sales.

While the interactive marketing world—be it the Internet, wireless platforms, or interactive television—has come under heavy fire from critics for being ineffective, I remain convinced that the interactive world is the first place a new company should spend its marketing dollars. This is assuming you have already established some type of direct sales mechanism and turned key early clients into marketing evangelists. Just as important, your company should continue to work diligently to lower the cost of deployment for your new product or service before even beginning the sales and marketing process. Your company should now turn to online marketing for its proven ability to stimulate direct customer response. In the words of CitySearch founder Charles Conn, Web marketing is about collapsing the distance between the creation of demand and its fulfillment.

Beware that, like so many marketers, you don't get caught up in the mentality of trying to turn the interactive world into something that it is not. The true beauty of interactive marketing is that it allows a potential customer to follow through on a specific marketing offer in real time and the company to track the effectiveness of the marketing offer, also in real time. This is a win-win situation for both parties.

It is helpful to think of Web marketing as working best at the bottom of a gigantic pyramid, where direct marketing reigns supreme, and being most ineffective at the top of the pyramid, where image-based advertising typically occurs. Given that most marketers come out of traditional advertising, their first reaction is to try to recreate imaged-based advertising online. This is what happened in the early Lexus television commercial cited by Charles Conn. The ad was so esoteric it didn't even feature an image of the car the company was trying to sell.

Image-intensive advertising online like the Lexus commercial is almost impossible to pull off. Yet this hasn't stopped many young startups from creating sizeable campaigns online that offer hugely wasteful brand-building experiments and no meaningful "call to action" for potential customers. Do whatever you must to avoid falling into this trap, even if it means withstanding some criticism from nervous investors and employees.

These naysayers will turn around and thank you when your sales and marketing operation is humming along nicely, and you don't have to decide whom to fire because a moronic "brand-building campaign" threw your entire operating budget out of whack! The interactive world can be your best friend for acquiring and retaining new customers if you think direct. Learn to love being a bottom feeder. Stay at the bottom of the marketing pyramid!

CHARLES CONN

Cofounder and Former Chairman of
TicketMasterCitySearch.com

Q **Ragas:** Industry analysts and traditional marketers regularly bash the Web as being largely ineffective as a sales and marketing medium. What lessons do you have for successful Web marketing and advertising?

A **Conn:** Let me first start with an imaginary pyramid. Up at the very tip of the pyramid is brand and image marketing. Down at the bottom is direct response—the promotional end of marketing— where you are giving things away, and you hope people take action right away. Do you remember those Lexus ads that appeared on television a few years go where it was only in the final seconds of the ad that you even saw the Lexus emblem? That Lexus commercial is at the far top of the pyramid. Giving people free tickets or free reservations to popular local music events or restaurants—that kind of marketing is at the bottom of the pyramid. What we have found here at CitySearch is that operating as close to the bottom of the pyramid as possible works best on the Web. People often say, "Oh my God! Why does banner advertising not work on the Web?" I tell them it's because a lot of the stuff that marketers try to do with banner advertising is a feeble imitation of that Lexus ad. They're trying to use that skinny little banner for the top end of the pyramid! It's really dumb!

Q **Ragas:** Right. There is no way at this point in the Web's evolution that marketers are able to effectively create very powerful image-based advertising online. Instead, they need to concentrate on direct response. You just can't force a square peg through a round hole!

A **Conn:** You can't do it. It just doesn't work! The visual medium of television is just so much more compelling for this kind of marketing. Maybe broadband will one day change this, but today the Web works best at the bottom of the pyramid. So digital companies should operate at a marketing level where people can interact immediately with their product or service, rather than try and create something that the consumer can take action on later. The way television works is that it

"Web marketing . . . is about collapsing the distance between creation of demand and satisfaction of demand."

creates a sense in your mind. You will watch that Lexus ad and say, "Oh my God. That Lexus is so beautiful. If I had that car, I would have access to that beauty." That's how television works. That's not how the Web works. Web marketing works best if a consumer can take action on something immediately. It's about collapsing the distance between creation of demand and satisfaction of demand. That's what the Web can do for you!

Don't Get Caught Napping

Assuming that you've learned to market successfully at the bottom of the pyramid and have turned all of your key customers into evangelists, you should now be well on your way towards creating a self-sufficient sales and marketing engine. However, it's at this point in time that your company will likely face big risks on the sales and marketing front. All too often, success breeds complacency and arrogance, which can spread like wildfire inside your organization and eat away at your company from the core. When this occurs, going from clear market leader to "yesterday's news" can happen almost within the blink of an eye. Fortunately, there are ways to quarantine these problems or to make sure that they never happen in the first place.

First, begin ingraining into your organization that sales and marketing are not exclusively the functions of your sales team and marketing department. Your accounting department and software engineers must learn to wear the sales hat as well. In a technology-focused business everyone in your company must participate in the sales and marketing process. Let's face it, a young growing business should always be selling—not just to the end customer—but to every stakeholder in the organization. In other words, if it moves, sell to it! I can assure you that if you're not constantly selling your ideas and vision to the press, industry analysts, and your investors, then someone else is selling theirs. So be prepared.

While rising above the clutter and noise in the marketplace is nice, it's staying there for good that's really the key. The only way to do that is to continuously stress to your entire company that the sales and marketing process is never really complete, as BroadVision founder Pehong Chen explains. There is no time to take a nap or daydream—there is only time to execute. Sales and marketing is not a process that only takes place out in the field or at the cramped desk of your marketing director. From mingling at dinner parties to chatting with new friends at a barbecue, the savvy employees of a digital business are always "selling" to the outside world. Learn to evangelize about your company's products and services to whoever will listen.

Sure, you can argue that this never-ending, 24/7 approach to sales and marketing sounds like we've created an obsessive group of people that spend far too much time on the job. Yet obsession screams passion, and passion is what energizes a market and potential customers. Rising above the clutter is never easy, but staying a few levels above the commotion for a sustainable period of time is really hard. That's why it takes seemingly extreme behavior to keep a market shook up and on edge today. A calm market is a complacent market, and complacent markets are ripe for being ignored and unnoticed by customers, as well as the media, industry analysts, private investors, and even public shareholders. That's why it's so important never to let your sales and marketing process rest. Sleep is for companies that have already dropped out of the race.

PEHONG CHEN

Chief Executive Officer, Chairman,
and Founder of BroadVision

Q **Ragas:** Typically, entrepreneurs and executives think of sales and marketing as only being important when their company is dealing with the actual end customer. What have you found to be the keys to effective sales and marketing in a high-tech organization?

A **Chen:** Today, we are in an extremely dynamic market where, if there is an opportunity, everyone quickly goes after it. The noise level is extremely high. To rise above the noise in the marketplace, entrepreneurs must do sales and marketing on almost every front. You must be constantly selling to your own employees, as well as analysts, the press, and ultimately, customers and investors. You have at least these four constituencies that you must always be selling to as a high-tech entrepreneur. You are basically selling every day! Once you can create an almost self-sufficient sales tornado, your job becomes a little easier, but in the high-tech business your job is never over!

> *"To rise above the noise in the marketplace, entrepreneurs must do sales and marketing on almost every front. You must constantly be selling!"*

Q **Ragas:** Yes. Companies must realize that today effective sales and marketing strategies must be intertwined into every facet of their organization. Companies should not be focused just on marketing and selling to their end customers, but also to every stakeholder in their organization.

A **Chen:** Initially, when you are an entrepreneur and starting from nothing, a lot of the sales and marketing process is devoted to convincing venture capitalists and your initial employees about the soundness and promise of your business. That's a heck of a sales job to begin with! After that, you have to start to educate the market, which includes analysts and customers. You then have to use sales and marketing to bring aboard early partner companies. If you eventually become a public company, a whole different set of constituencies come on the scene. This is a very interesting business where your sales and marketing job is never really done. It can be fun, but also very challenging!

CHAPTER 5

BUILDING A MEANINGFUL E-BRAND

SOME THINGS NEVER REALLY CHANGE, ESPECIALLY THE POWER of brand names and branding. As long ago as the Egyptians, people were using brands to signify ownership of livestock. On the American frontier, ownership brands became also a symbol of great pride for ranchers. Texas cattlemen often named their ranches after their brand and even displayed their branding mark on the gateposts to their ranches. Make no mistake: Brands not only served as imaginary fences on the frontier but also became the equivalent of a knight's coat of arms. Whether you were a cattle rancher of 150 years ago or are a digital business starting up today, you live or die by the power of your brand name.

Just as the cattle brand was key to ownership in a business in which ownership was everything, a company's brand today serves an important purpose. A brand is so much more than

Nike's swoosh logo or the signature Ralph Lauren polo horse. Brands are not static logos or symbols to be put on the cover of a company's marketing package. A brand is a company's living soul and is representative of every facet of the company's business. A company's brand is like a piece of clay being constantly shaped, formed, and resculpted by every interaction a customer has with the organization. The building of a strong and enduring brand is a serious part of forming your company. It is not an overnight process, and it can be fraught with risk.

Let's take a look back at the pioneering Texas cattlemen and their famous branding irons. Ranchers who overheated their irons ran the real risk of burning their cattle and leaving on them an open sore that could become infected. However, if the iron was not hot enough, it burned slowly and painfully, and the steer's hair would re-grow over the brand. These same issues of not applying enough heat to a company's brand or burning a brand to smithereens with too much heat and clumsy product or service positioning still very much exist today. The number of misconceptions surrounding brand building is staggering. Even bricks and mortar companies seem to struggle with the best ways to protect and nurture their brands when they decide to go online. In this chapter I will give you an easy-to-follow process for building and then nurturing a brand in the digital realm. Glen Meakem of FreeMarkets and Launch Media founder Dave Goldberg will share with us the importance of a company first building a truly great product or service that offers a superior value proposition. Without clearing this first hurdle, a great new brand has no chance of being created.

Next, we will explore with MightyWords.com chairman Chris MacAskill the realization that simply creating a killer new product or service by itself isn't enough to get noticed in today's crowded market. An organization must do everything in its power to never allow its brand to be ignored.

With this in mind, I will suggest ways for your company to develop a brand, as well as products or services, which spread by "word-of-mouse," or virally, as Vicinity CEO Emerick Woods explains. We will then focus on the importance of taking a "bottoms-up" approach to branding as a way to increase a company's chance of success, with the help of Go2Net founder Russell Horowitz. Finally, Powered founder Michael Rosenfelt will explain why the digital world is only one slice of the overall brand-building pie. Savvy e-brands always find a way to make the bricks-and-mortar world their best friend.

Welcome to the Age of Commoditization

The first thing that technology companies as well as existing bricks-and-mortar businesses must understand is that, in the age of the Internet, buyers are amassing more power over sellers than ever before. Buyers no longer find themselves fumbling in the dark about a product or service and at the mercy of a salesperson for unbiased information. The Web community has now become its own living and breathing *Consumer Reports* magazine. In pre-Internet days, buyers might talk among a handful of friends and colleagues before making a purchase. Post-Internet buyers now browse hundreds of search engines, discussions lists, and comparison-shopping engines for detailed insights on a product or service before making a decision.

This shift in power from sellers to buyers is especially important as it relates to brands, because it suggests that we are entering an Age of Commoditization that will prove fatal to brands that don't offer a superior value proposition. Companies that have nonchalantly slapped their existing widely regarded brand name on inferior new products or services are becoming history. Customers will know faster than ever before when you are lying and trying to pass off a cheap imitation as the real thing. For example, unless Microsoft offers a mouse that is superior or at least equal to similar products offered by a competitor like Logitech, then it will likely find in the future that it will have lost all ability to charge higher prices than its rivals.

I'm not trying to single out Microsoft here, but there are a number of blue-chip tech names ranging from Hewlett Packard to IBM that have coasted for years now, using their existing brand recognition to expand into new product categories. This "brand coasting" will likely turn very quickly into an uncontrollable nosedive unless these companies are very careful. Unhappy digital customers eat dishonest brands for breakfast. That's why it's so crucial for companies to build superior products and services that are truly differentiated and superior to the competition. Otherwise, you will find yourself trying to build a brand that is never able to gain traction, because consumers will know you're trying to pull a fast one on them.

The Internet doesn't lie. It always finds a way to bring to the surface the voices that tell the truth. If your product or service stinks worse than a frightened skunk, the whole world is going to hear about it—and fast. All the advertising and public relations spinning in the world won't be able to save you. As FreeMarkets CEO Glen Meakem points out, companies that are simply in the business of milking a brand created long ago are in a heap of trouble in this coming Age of Commoditization. On the upside, companies that understand this shifting of the power scale among buyers and sellers are being presented with incredible brand-building opportunities. Offer a superior value proposition, and you'll win—time and time again. It's that simple.

GLEN MEAKEM

Founder, Chairman, and
Chief Executive Officer of FreeMarkets

Q **Ragas:** Pundits are claiming that the proliferation of the Internet and new online marketplaces will mark the eventual devaluation of most brands. What should companies do to protect and insulate their brands?

A **Meakem:** The bottom line is that since 1994 incredible global brands like Yahoo and eBay have been created. So it's still possible to create a new brand, and brands still have tremendous value. We have to recognize that the world we're in right now is one in which buyers are getting better and better information and becoming more and more intelligent. So the power is shifting. What the Internet means fundamentally is that power is shifting from sellers to buyers. This shifting of power is especially true at the retail level. Buyers of all kinds of things can now go on the Net and comparison shop for cars, books, and a thousand other items. At the same time, industrial buyers can use new kinds of e-markets to comparison shop their suppliers. So the brand name of an information source channel like Yahoo, eBay, or FreeMarkets becomes incredibly valuable, because it is the branded portal that people trust.

> *"What the Internet means fundamentally is that the power is shifting from sellers to buyers."*

Q **Ragas:** We are definitely in a digital world where the buyer has more power and leverage over the seller than ever before. So trusted information-based products and services should actually find their brands enhanced in this new environment.

A **Meakem:** However, if a brand simply supports a manufactured item that has similar qualities to competing products, then that brand is eventually going to be devalued! Brands are still valuable, but it must be the right brand in a defensible space. I used to work on the Jell-O gelatin line a long time ago when I was with Kraft Foods. Jell-O can still premium price versus Royal gelatin and private label gelatins because of the Jell-O brand name. I believe that's a bad place to be long term, because the only real value in Jell-O is in the brand. That's all there is! The underlying products are equivalent in every other way. What a company needs is a brand that supports a value proposition that is superior and differentiated. If you're in the business of just milking the value of a brand created long ago, you're in trouble in a commoditizing world.

Want a Great Brand?
Build a Great Product or Service!

As companies come to grips with the harsh realities of the Age of Commoditization, it is becoming increasingly clear that great brands begin and end with the building of great products and services. The two clearly go hand in hand. Somehow, though, the last few years have lulled many tech executives into thinking that shelling out millions upon million of dollars on Super Bowl ads and sponsorships of professional sports stadiums can serve as some sort of substitute. A pricey spokesperson, a catchy marketing slogan, and a barrage of advertisements are no longer enough to hide a company's inferior product or service. You will be found out and promptly shot by consumers. Brands are not built on the backs of brute marketing force. They never have been, and they never will be.

While online retailing giant Amazon.com has spent hundreds of millions on marketing, the real reason the company is a great brand name today is because it offers arguably the most enjoyable customer experience on the Web. Amazon.com chairman Jeff Bezos and his team remain fanatical about providing incredible individual service to every single one of their company's customers. That is really what has built Amazon's incredible brand today. If brand building was simply about luring customers with deep price discounts and other marketing offers, competitors like Borders Books and Barnes & Noble would be eating Amazon for lunch by now. They aren't.

The same goes for Linux giant, Red Hat Software. While founders Bob Young and Marc Ewing's wearing of snazzy red hats at every press opportunity certainly didn't hurt the company's brand-building efforts, the Red Hat brand was really built by consistently delivering top-notch Linux and open-source software solutions to customers. Web-portal company Yahoo followed a similar brand-creation path. Yahoo founders Jerry Yang and David Filo built a great service first—in this case a search engine—and then leveraged this superior service and a loyal customer base into the makings of an internationally recognized media brand.

When you boil it all down, the key to brand building is quite simple. Customers will always flock to quality and reliability in superior and differentiated products and services. As a boatload of bankrupt dot-coms can now attest, the biggest advertising blitz in the world can't turn a subpar company into a meaningful brand. In the end, it will be your customers—not your marketing department or advertising agency—that decide the fate of your brand, as Launch Media founder Dave Goldberg points out. You must at least start out on the right foot: Develop a solid foundation for your new brand by first offering your customers a unique and superior value proposition.

While customers may forget your latest marketing jingle by the time they get off the couch, they'll almost always remember a great product or service.

David Goldberg

Founder, Chief Executive Officer,
and Chairman of Launch Media

Q **Ragas:** Building a new brand from scratch is never easy or a process that can be done overnight. So what have you learned are the keys to really creating and nurturing a tech company's name into a widely recognizable e-brand?

A **Goldberg:** If you look at the online brands that have been really successful, even to a certain degree Amazon.com, it's really all about building a great product or service along with great user experience. That is what really generates the great brand over the long term. Think about it. Yahoo spends basically nothing on brand advertising. How many Internet companies ran ads last year at Christmastime where we even remember the ad now? If you're not using a dot-com's product or service, it doesn't matter if they're spending $20 million dollars, $50 million dollars, or even $100 million dollars. There's no particular value to a brand if a customer doesn't value the experience. This is not to say that a company can't do some kind of brand advertising to accelerate customer knowledge, but it's more of an added "topping." Brand advertising shouldn't be the core of your branding strategy. The core of your branding strategy should be to build a great product or service and then figure out how to get customers to use it.

> *"There's no particular value to a brand if a customer doesn't value the experience."*

Don't Allow Your Brand to Be Ignored

Even with a great product or service, your company will still likely face an uphill battle in the brand-building wars. Even if you've reached the top of the hill, your customers will be assailed by pressure sales pitches, customer testimonials, money-back guarantees, and other marketing missiles lobbed by your competitors. I'm sure you've felt this same feeling before yourself—overwhelmed and out of breath—which is a situation ripe for brand erosion and confusion. That's why organizations must do whatever it takes to make sure that their brands are never ignored. It's not that customers will necessarily forget your brand in a crowded marketplace, but every nudge and helpful reminder that says, "I'm still here!" really helps.

Think about the last baseball game or sporting event that you attended. Which vendor was selling the most from his tray? Was it the tireless guy working the aisles back and forth yelling, "Cold beer here!" or was it the timid fellow standing back in the stands holding the tray of fresh peanuts and popcorn and wondering why he has no customers? You see what I mean. You can have the greatest product or service in the world—maybe even the world's greatest peanuts and popcorn—but if no one is reminded that your brand exists, then it really doesn't matter. Often, out of sight equals out of mind. That's why smart companies always find a way to keep their brand constantly in the public eye, as MightyWords.com chief Chris MacAskill will remind us.

Regardless of what you really think of someone like flamboyant retired basketball star Dennis Rodman or flashy real estate baron Donald Trump, one has to admit that neither of these two people ever allow their brands to be ignored. The same goes for semiconductor kingpin Intel Corporation. It wouldn't have been hard for consumers to forget that Intel's chips go into virtually every PC sold. Talk about having a very real risk of brand erosion. Here's a product that the vast majority of customers will never even see! So what did Intel do? It made sure that an "Intel Inside" sticker was slapped onto the outside of every single computer sold. And who today can forget Intel's catchy five-note signature tune at the end of every one of its television commercials?

This is the essence of never allowing your company's brand to be ignored!

CHRIS MACASKILL

Founder and Chairman of FatBrain.com;
Chief Executive Officer of MightyWords.com

Q **Ragas:** Seemingly, every company is interested in enhancing the value and visibility of its brand. However, shelling out millions on additional advertising typically isn't the answer. What advice do you have for getting a company's product or service noticed?

A **MacAskill:** I was profoundly influenced on the topic of branding by a talk that Amazon.com founder Jeff Bezos gave at Stanford University that I had attended. Bezos told us how, after introducing user-generated reviews on Amazon's site, he found the books that sold the best were getting either one-star or five-star reviews. The books that received average ratings of three to four stars simply don't sell well. His point was that these sales results on Amazon prove yet again that the only real problem in life is to be ignored. When I heard that, I thought, Of course. My first company, FatBrain.com, was named Computer Literacy at the time, which is probably the most forgettable name imaginable. I walked out of Stanford thinking that Jeff Bezos was right: The only real problem in life is to be ignored. So I decided that we

> *"Most people are too comfortable doing things in standard business practice like everyone else. The companies that really get all the attention are the ones who are different."*

weren't going to select a brand name that allows us to be ignored. I think most people are too comfortable doing things using standard business practice like everyone else. The companies who get all the attention are the ones who are different. For example, Steve Jobs at Apple Computers. He makes plastic see-through computers, is temperamental, and wears black turtlenecks. He's always in the news for something, because he just doesn't allow himself to be ignored.

Think "Word-of-Mouse"

Not only must you never allow your company's brand to be ignored, you must absolutely make sure it is inherently viral in nature. Your solution should instantly knock the socks off your customers, to the extent that they immediately go out and tell everyone they know about it! Nothing builds and sustains a brand quicker than a new product or service that is so unique and awe-inspiring that its very usage spreads the word about it like a virus. Communication products like Palm Inc.'s wildly popular Palm Pilot line of handheld devices and Research In Motion's Blackberry pager are both prime examples of relatively young products that built their brands primarily through customer-propelled viral marketing.

As I have stated throughout this chapter, creating great brands comes down to first creating great new products and services. If Palm and Research In Motion had both initially released run-of-the-mill communication tools that were similar to products already on the market, it is unlikely that their brands would mean much of anything to the reader of this book today. Truly killer brands represent companies with products and services that are so mind-blowing and different that one can't help but tell their friends, neighbors, relatives, and colleagues about what they purchased. These are the brands that customers say they just can't live without!

Think about this viral phenomenon some more for a second. This infectious desire to tell a friend about an exciting new product or service is amplified by the interconnected nature of the Web. Combine the Web and viral and you may have just found the Holy Grail to brand building. Word-of-mouse marketing among friends is largely responsible for the evolution of once fledgling tech startups like eBay, Yahoo, Netscape, and Napster into incredible global brands today. In essence, these are brands that have found real ways to create products or services for the people and by the people. This is something that even the largest Madison Avenue ad agencies can never replicate for a competitor, no matter how hard they try, as Vicinity CEO Emerick Woods explains.

Digital companies are no longer in an operating environment that will support a traditional marketing-intensive approach to brand building. The patience of investors and the capital markets towards entrepreneurs who spend piles of their precious cash for the "greater good of brand building" is history. This leaves young companies with only two choices if they are really serious about building a mainstream brand: Get viral and find a way to quickly incite "click-to-mouse" brand building. If you don't, the brand will die before it's even born.

Companies must either create a new product or service that is so groundbreaking and different that it invokes instant excitement in customers, or else realize that this will never happen and quickly shelve their brand-building dreams. There really is no in-between if you want your company to be a survivor!

EMERICK WOODS

Chief Executive Officer and President of Vicinity; former Chief Executive Officer and President of TuneUp.com

Q **Ragas:** Over the past year, the market has largely destroyed the myth that hundreds of powerful new brands can be spawned from the tech sector. What can new companies do to increase the chances that they will end up as one of the next great e-brands?

A **Woods:** I personally believe that the number of New Economy brands that will be created will actually be fairly small. There will be eBay, Amazon, Yahoo, and a few others. I think that unless a company's product or service is something that is inherently "viral" in nature, it is extremely difficult to create a mainstream brand. An example of a brand that was clearly formed virally by word of mouth was eBay. To some extent, Yahoo was the same way. Relevant to their size and their revenue base, Yahoo has never spent heavily on building their brand. AOL did spend a lot of money building its brand. Instant-messaging company Mirabilis, the creator of ICQ, didn't spend anything. They didn't spend a dime on marketing, and now they've got tens of millions—if not somewhere north of a hundred million—users! Almost every Internet user now knows about ICQ's instant messaging and chat software. One of the things I often say is that most of the New Economy brands will eventually become Old Economy brands. To some extent, that's starting to come true. Certainly, there will still be some new brands created, but I think that, by and large, it's going to be ones that already exist. I think that a lot of successful new business models like Ariba and Commerce One are going to be based around companies that provide the infrastructure to existing brands.

> *"I think that unless a company's product or service is inherently 'viral' in nature, it is extremely difficult to create a mainstream brand."*

Practice "Bottoms-Up" Branding

Once you have developed a viral brand, it is extremely important that your brand remains keenly focused (at least initially) on supporting a particular product set or service. Otherwise, your company's brand runs the risk of becoming watered down and stretched out of shape in the consumer's mind. Confusion will almost always kill the golden goose. Cast a net with your brand that is initially very focused. Don't allow your company to become a fisherman hoping to get lucky by casting a wide net in treacherous seas.

One of the easiest ways to cast this "focused net" is for your company to take a "bottoms-up" approach to branding. In many regards, this goes counter to the "top-down" route, which typically calls for heavy marketing expenditures over an extended period of time. Moving from the top down, a company begins applying its brand to a widening array of products and services. British entrepreneur Richard Branson's Virgin Inc. is a perfect example of this strategy in practice. The Virgin brand today can be found slapped on everything from airplanes and trains to music and soft drinks.

While a top-down strategy can work in the traditional business world, it typically fails miserably in the more time-compressed digital business environment. Technology-focused organizations simply don't have the time or required capital to establish their brand in the marketplace using this buckshot philosophy. As we have repeatedly seen, the majority of the most successful Next Economy brands have originated to date with companies that initially launched a very targeted product or service. Even e-commerce giant Amazon.com began its business by initially targeting only one particular product category—books—before moving into additional categories.

By following this pinpoint approach to brand building, you will find it enables your company to devote more time to focusing on the creation, distribution, and sales of your product or service. As I have mentioned throughout this chapter, the most powerful brands are created by customers (not companies) and the actual experience these customers have with your products or services. Don't allow your firm to fall into the trap of trying to put the cart before the horse or, in this case, the brand before the value proposition.

As Go2Net founder Russell Horowitz points out, in today's crowded marketplace a bottoms-up approach to branding offers the highest probability for success and ensures that a company spends more time improving customer satisfaction than trying to practice ill-fated, ad-driven "brand-building alchemy."

RUSSELL HOROWITZ
Founder and Former Chairman of Go2Net, Inc.

Q **Ragas:** It is becoming increasingly difficult for new technology-focused companies to develop a brand that sticks in the mind of customers and really matters. What advice do you have about the best way for new companies to approach the brand-building process?

A **Horowitz:** There are a couple of ways to go about the brand-building process. One way is to look at it from a traditional perspective, which means that a company must spend massive amounts on marketing over extended periods. The technology industry just doesn't afford you the opportunity to do that kind of marketing anymore. There are exceptions, but those companies can be counted on one hand. For every company that succeeded with the traditional approach, there were thousands and thousands that failed. What we focused on instead at Go2Net was to really look at the product or service and the utility that it gave to the end user. The actual brand became secondary, and that's why I've historically characterized our strategy as "bottoms-up," as opposed to the more traditional approach in building a brand, which is from the top down.

Q **Ragas:** You're suggesting that in today's market with access to capital not as plentiful as it once was, new companies simply don't have the time and money to build brands in the traditional way. A bottoms-up approach is much more feasible now than a top-down approach to brand building.

A **Horowitz:** The top-down approach is to establish the brand, make the brand important, and then develop complimentary products or services that the brand supports. The extreme example is probably Virgin Inc. Virgin went from records to airlines and all sorts of other products. Products and services are simply a "moving target" for these kinds of companies. They're probably not still selling the same products they began with, and next week they'll probably be creating something else. Yahoo really did that. It developed from a Web directory into a portal that eventually offered more and more across-the-board services. What we did instead was to focus on the product or service first, and then we built the brand on the back of it. The top-down approach isn't impossible, but if you were looking at where opportunities are today I'd put that

> *"The top-down approach isn't impossible . . . but I'd put that one in the category of 'don't touch it with a ten-foot pole!'"*

one in the category of "don't touch it with a ten-foot pole!" That's not to say that some companies can't pull it off, but the reality is that the technology business is a function of risk-reward. So you have to assess what gives you the best probability of success.

Brand with a Laser Beam

By embarking on a "bottoms-up" approach to brand creation, your company should find it easier to capture a clearly defined and defensible position in the customer's mind. One step at a time works. Be patient. After all, any great warrior nation, ranging from the ancient Romans to the Klingons from *Star Trek*, built their empires one step at a time in a very focused and systematic fashion. The Klingons didn't try to take over the entire universe in just one weekend! They expanded outward over time, picking up slices of the galaxy along the way. Creating, growing, and then defending a really strong brand isn't very different from the Klingons' plan for conquest.

As you conduct your brand-building mission, use an almost laser-beam focus. It is important to remember that the Internet is only one instrument in the entire branding symphony. While the interactive realm is an extremely powerful medium for conducting effective sales and marketing, the fact remains that even the most successful technology-driven companies have eventually ventured offline to enhance the value of their brands. Even mega-brand Yahoo copublishes its own monthly print magazine in the form of the very successful *Yahoo! Internet Life*. And don't forget that online brokerage giant E*TRADE established its own bricks-and-mortar presence by purchasing the third largest ATM network in the United States.

While the Web is a very important instrument in the brand-building symphony, there are also a myriad number of other flutes and violins that tech-driven companies can utilize to more effectively interact with their customers. As Powered founder Michael Rosenfelt notes, we really don't live all of our lives on the Web! The more "touch points" beyond the Web that you can establish with customers, the better the chance that your brand will leave a lasting impression in their minds.

Of course, this multi-channel approach can only work if your product or service clearly offers a superior value proposition and delivers a phenomenal customer experience. Otherwise, you are probably wasting your time by venturing beyond the digital realm.

MICHAEL ROSENFELT

Founder of Powered, Inc.; Venture Partner, Impact Venture Partners

Q **Ragas:** Obviously, every technology-focused company today is on a quest to build its brand as quickly as possible. Does this compression of time change the way that digital companies should go about developing their brands?

A **Rosenfelt:** Things that you need to do to build a brand for a technology company are the same things fundamentally that you need to build a brand, period. You have to start with the basics. In other words, what is the problem you're trying to solve? Specifically, how do you position your company and its product or service to solve that problem? Classic positioning of a company involves asking simple questions like, Who are we? Who do we want to be when we grow up? How do we want to be perceived by our customers? In other words, companies must decide what mental rung they want to own in the minds of their customers. By doing this, a company can get a really narrow, laser-beam focus on defining what position in the marketplace they're trying to own. It will then become much easier for the company to cut through the clutter and begin to establish a brand position that resonates in the market. Building a brand is not about advertising, and it's not about marketing stunts. Those things are tools. Establishing the very essence of what a company does and its position in the marketplace is how you really build a brand.

Q **Ragas:** So a company must first envision exactly how it wants its product or service to be remembered by its customers. Until an organization does this, it is destined to have trouble properly positioning its brand.

A **Rosenfelt:** Bricks-and-mortar businesses, and most technology companies, need to understand that the Web is just another form of communication and distribution. The Web is just another aspect of a customer-company relationship. In many respects, except for eBay where the Web is the network and the company's business, people forget that the Web is only part of the customer's experience. There are a number of other vehicles to "touch" and "feel" a customer. It would be very myopic to think about the Web as the exclusive vehicle for communicating a brand with customers.

"It would be very myopic to think about the Web as the exclusive vehicle for communicating a brand with customers."

Think about marketing as a symphony in terms of the different communications vehicles you can use to interact with customers. In other words, the Web may be a very important instrument, but there are a whole host of other instruments in that symphony that all have to play the concert together to be effective. Essentially, what you ultimately want is full stereophonic sound from multiple speakers on your customer. The Web is just one part. We don't live our lives on the Web as much as we in technology like to think we do.

CHAPTER 6

BUILDING MIND SHARE AND CUSTOMER LOYALTY

GRAB CUSTOMER MIND SHARE, REACH CRITICAL MASS, AND achieve long-term customer loyalty. This is the Holy Trinity of customer relationship management for every digital and bricks-and-mortar company. It is this trio that separates the long-term survivor from the short-term flameout in the technology world.

Surprisingly, the formula for building and sustaining this mind-share–critical-mass–loyalty cycle in your own business is waiting for you right inside your refrigerator! Stick your head in and take a good look. What you'll likely find is a familiar array of food brands ranging from Velveeta cheese slices and Oscar-Meyer cold cuts to Heinz ketchup and French's mustard. Over the years, each of these companies has grabbed mind share, translated it into critical mass, and ended up with exceedingly high customer loyalty. Think about it. Chances are that, week after week, you purchase exactly the same brands of ketchup and sliced cheese without even realizing it!

While brand name food companies may not be the world's most innovative corporations, they generally do an excellent job of manufacturing a consistent, quality product. But if food companies were like some Web and technology companies, they would ship foods to your grocery store that were spoiled, tasted funny, or were out of stock on the shelves! That doesn't usually happen, because most of the major brand food companies are experts at building critical mass for a product, and then, in most cases, creating a sense of undying loyalty in their customer base. Just look at how violently consumers reacted back in 1985 when Coca-Cola tried to introduce the New Coke formula!

Technology companies that can achieve this same high level of mind share, critical mass, and high customer loyalty and passion have an incredible long-term advantage over their competition. In this chapter I will explore with you how companies can follow a path to grab focused customer mind share, which in turn can be translated into critical mass for a company's product or service. Later on in the chapter, we will focus on how organizations can enhance and maintain high customer loyalty for their product or service. After all, hitting critical mass means very little by itself if the net result is that you have only created an expensive revolving door for your customers.

Venture capitalist Harry Motro and PRIMEDIA head Tom Rogers will then share with us the importance of having focus when trying to capture mind share, as well as the importance of organically building rather than "renting" a customer base. We will see that, without customer mind share and organically grown critical mass, a company has little hope of achieving a significant level of customer loyalty.

Fortunately, there are ways to speed up a company's path to organic critical mass, as Cobalt Group founder John Holt will explain.

After critical mass has been fully explored, we will delve into ways to boost customer loyalty and close the "revolving door," with Think New Ideas founder Scott Mednick and VerticalNet chairman Mark Walsh. Yet all this work on rapidly grabbing mind share and building critical mass is for naught unless a company continues to open its ears to the constantly changing desires of its customer base. Former IBM executive John Schwartz will end this chapter by providing us with firsthand advice on ways companies can maintain high customer lock-in over the long haul.

Mind Share Is All About Focus

Today's crowded tech marketplace does not allow fledgling young companies to dive into the customer pool, do a belly flop, and splash water everywhere. You can try this approach, but it won't be enough to get your product or service noticed. The pool is so crowded today that no one will likely even hear the splash of your company's entry into the water. Unfocused splashes in the form of scattershot marketing, public relations, and customer segmentation will fall mostly on deaf ears. Particularly if your product or service is not vastly superior to solutions already available from the competition!

Effectively capturing customer mind share today requires focus. Targeted surgical air strikes—not scorch-the-earth bombing runs—win. Be like a Stealth fighter pilot and focus your efforts on a specific customer segment. Focus on a particular marketing and P.R. message. Focus on delivering one tried and true value proposition to your customers. Most important, though, focus on delivering an incredibly high level of consistency and reliability within your product or service. Nothing erodes a company's mind share faster than a tech product or service that breaks the reliability and consistency promise.

Going back to my earlier analogy of food manufacturers, how long do you think Frito-Lay would remain the world's leading snack food company if every fourth bag of Doritos tasted like Cheetos? Or every tenth bag? Not very long! Customers would be angry, and their loyalty would likely fall off a cliff almost overnight. Think of the vast number of tech companies that regularly don't deliver as promised! The customer's reaction: I expected your software might crash, but not this often!

Grabbing mind share in the marketplace is not an overnight process. If you can't keep a consistent and long-term focus, you may have to retreat to safety after only a few skirmishes in the field. Without focus and guaranteed reliability of their products or services, young companies are probably just as well off marketing to themselves all day long in a padded cell. In the real estate business, the motto is: Location, Location, Location. Grabbing that initial slice of customer mind share in the technology business is all about Focus, Focus, Focus, as venture capitalist Harry Motro relates.

HARRY MOTRO

Chairman of MotroVentures;
former Chief Executive Officer of Infoseek/GO.com

Q **Ragas:** The digital universe today is chock full of companies offering seemingly dozens of related products and services. What is really the key for these companies as they try to capture substantial mind share and reach critical mass?

A **Motro:** One of the keys to achieving true critical mass is to clearly define what exactly you're trying to take over. When people say that they are trying to capture mind share and that they want to "own" a consumer's mind, I always think that no one really owns Harry Motro's mind. I can have a relationship with a particular company and their product or service, but you still don't own my mind. My relationship with a company is going to be based on a very specific benefit to me. The early days when companies blundered into the Web, as almost all of the early players did, are entirely over. It's really hard today to reach critical mass. There's just so much noise out there! I think the opportunity for companies today to capture mind share is to narrowly and clearly target what messages they are putting out there to their customers. What do you really want to focus on? In the real estate business, they say it's all about Location, Location, Location.

> *"The opportunity for companies today to capture mind share is to narrowly and clearly target what messages they are putting out there."*

Well, messaging, getting mind share, and then establishing a long-lasting relationship with a tech customer today is all about Focus, Focus, and Focus!

Borrowing Customers Never Works

Even companies that do understand the importance of a laser-beam focus when capturing mind share often fool themselves into believing there is a quick and easy way to cut corners on the way to reaching critical mass. The only thing "quick and easy" about this process is how quickly and easily young companies can burn through all of their capital on this quest. As the last few years have so brutally demonstrated, the path to critical mass is one that has no shortcuts and is full of potential pitfalls.

Perhaps nowhere in the tech sector was this more evident than with DrKoop.com, the e-health Web site started by former Surgeon General C. Everett Koop. After a successful $84 million initial public offering in June of 1999, the company's management became convinced it needed to partner with a number of high-profile portal sites in order to rapidly grow its membership base. Soon thereafter, DrKoop.com signed a staggering four-year $89 million marketing alliance with America Online. As the months ticked by after the deal was announced, it became clear to investors that, instead of quickening the company's path to critical mass, the deal actually ended up nearly bankrupting the company!

Trying to grab mind share and reach critical mass by "renting" someone else's customers—in this case AOL's—simply doesn't work. Become an owner, not a renter. Build your customer base organically. While most tech companies today have learned their lessons after cutting expensive "portal deals," some firms are still shelling out millions of dollars on alliances with traditional media and bricks and mortar companies. While these deals don't always fail, the chances of ever seeing real customer loyalty from "borrowed customers" are virtually nil until your company has created a superior and differentiated product or service. As I mentioned earlier in this chapter, critical mass without corresponding customer loyalty leads to a revolving door syndrome that forces companies to constantly churn through customers. It's a bit like running in the same place for three hours trying to win the Boston marathon. It's a valiant effort, but it's not going to get you anywhere. That's why it's crucial that you explore ways to build direct relationships with your customers instead of trying to co-opt customers through third parties. Finding innovative ways to stimulate word of mouth among the initial customer base continues to be the most effective strategy to reach and sustain critical mass, according to former NBC Cable president Tom Rogers.

TOM ROGERS

Chairman and Chief Executive Officer of PRIMEDIA
Inc.; former President of NBC Cable

Q **Ragas:** One factor that has handicapped a lot of digital companies, as well as offline firms, is that they have all done a lousy job on the customer-retention aspect of their business. Do you have any advice on how to increase customer loyalty?

A **Rogers:** The notion of trying to build a business by leveraging off a brand that doesn't belong to you isn't the way to do it! Don't try to build a business by piggybacking on another brand, such as paying America Online or Yahoo tons of money to "rent" their online traffic or even paying traditional companies like us to cross-promote. This isn't the way to do it! Online media company About.com is a good example of a company that has largely avoided having the noose of consumer marketing expenses placed around its neck. They found a way to grab customers through viral marketing without paying other people huge amounts of money to borrow their customers! I believe that existing companies that already have built-in audiences should use marketing and promotion as a key part of this equation, but they should

> *"The notion of trying to build a business by leveraging off of a brand that doesn't belong to you isn't the way to do it!"*

do so in a way that builds other aspects of the business. Which means that companies shouldn't underestimate things like a product or service's quality, the word of mouth it generates among customers, and how this effect multiplies as you hang onto loyal customers. It is very difficult to instantaneously drive your business if you don't have a unique proposition that is truly different from the marketplace. First mover advantage worked for a select few companies like Yahoo, AOL, and eBay. If you're not one of them, though, your company needs a better formula for acquiring customers than thinking you can borrow someone else's. You can't create a unique product or service by spending a lot of money borrowing someone else's customers.

Win Support from Key Industry Influencers

While trying to rent or borrow another company's customers is usually a bad idea, there is a way to speed up the process of reaching critical mass. First, you will need to identify the key influencers in your industry—well-known media personalities, highly regarded industry analysts, business organizations, and market-leading corporations—and then start to court them. Make your approach to these key industry influencers as early as possible and work hard to win them over as loyal customers. If your value proposition is really as good as you think it is, these organizations or individuals often can be turned into valuable evangelists for your product or service.

The favorable opinion these influencers have of your product or service, together with their built-in following and the respect with which they are held, can play a huge role in helping your company do a fast grab of mind share and reach critical mass. For proof of how this works, just look at how many new books recommended by mega-talk-show-host Oprah Winfrey have regularly shot to the top of the bestseller list!

Building a company's customer base by utilizing this influencer strategy is not the same as renting or borrowing customers from other companies. What influencers do is provide you with a favorable and personalized introduction into their sphere of influence. It then becomes your company's job to convince these followers that your product or service is worthy of their hard-earned dollars. Let's face it, industry influencers can open doors for you, but they can't build customer loyalty for your business. When this strategy is leveraged properly, as Cobalt Group CEO John Holt found out, it can drastically reduce the time it takes for a company to reach and sustain critical mass.

JOHN HOLT

Chief Executive Officer and
Founder of The Cobalt Group

Q **Ragas:** Let's assume that a company already understands that it must focus on one specific target market if its hopes to gain mind share and reach critical mass. Beyond having this laser-beam focus, what else can companies due to stimulate the critical mass process?

A **Holt:** Our strategy was pretty specific to the automotive industry, but there are a couple of lessons that any company can take away from our experience. Because we were initially self-funded, we could not go to the 20,000 car dealers in the country one by one and try to sign them up for our services. We just didn't have the money to do it. So we settled on a strategy of offering services car manufacturers desired, and this in turn created an endorsement from them and introduced us into their dealer networks. It was a very leverageable strategy of reaching critical mass. It ended up being enormous for us! The way it worked was, let's say that all of a sudden Toyota selects Cobalt. During their dealer conference to introduce their new cars, Toyota assigns Cobalt a booth at no cost, because Toyota wants its dealers to have Web sites and use our services!

Q **Ragas:** So a company early on in its product or service's life cycle should go out and do whatever it takes to win the business and support of major influencers in the industry. Winning over these industry influencers is the key to rapidly hitting critical mass.

A **Holt:** In our business it was pretty easy to segment the major influencers in our market, because there are maybe only twenty or twenty-five manufacturers. But I would say that market segmentation is very important for any company trying to reach critical mass. Obviously, in our case, all manufacturer endorsements were powerful. It didn't matter if the manufacturer was Hyundai or General Motors. Something else that we did that was pretty smart was to work for the auto manufacturers at very low costs in return for those early endorsements. Basically, we took a look at the business risks and said, "I bet that if we win that manufacturer's endorsement we'll also win its dealers." I believe this is a sensible strategy to follow, but you must be willing to do some discounting early on to build up your business with it.

"I would say that market segmentation is very important for any company trying to reach critical mass."

There's No Critical Mass Without Customer Loyalty

As you've already heard me say repeatedly throughout this chapter, the revolving door syndrome kills companies. Dozens upon dozens of the Internet startups that went belly-up over the past two years were forced to shut their doors because their customer retention strategy was no more effective than stopping water running through a sieve. Without customer loyalty, achieving critical mass is a waste of time. Most businesses are not sustainable if the organization is constantly churning through customers and always trying to lure a new batch of customers through the door.

Neither Web infrastructure companies Cisco Systems and Exodus Communications nor consumer Internet firms like Amazon.com and America Online would still exist today if all four didn't experience an exceedingly high level of customer loyalty. How did these companies all master the third piece of the mind-share–critical-mass–customer loyalty trinity? Simple. They consistently built superior and reliable products and services with a clear value proposition. These companies weren't just focused on closing a sale—they were just as interested in creating a satisfied loyal customer in the process.

Although it doesn't take a rocket scientist to figure out that satisfied customers typically turn into loyal customers, the tech marketplace is still chock full of companies that are only concerned with acquiring more users and making quick sales. They are not concerned with improving either the quality of the product or service or the complete customer experience they provide. Look at the corpses of failed e-tail operations like Furniture.com, MotherNature.com, and ValueAmerica, none of whom could consistently fill and ship orders on time. Over-promising and under-delivering almost always kills!

Let's consider as an example how over-promising and under-delivering affects a professional sports franchise that spends millions of dollars to fill its stadium with curious fans during its first season. If the team plays badly and the season ends up a big disappointment, this organization is essentially still at square one. They may even have gone backward a few squares, because thousands of fans are now in the sports bars telling everyone they know how lousy the team is and how mad they are!

As Think New Ideas founder Scott Mednick reminds us, companies must understand the difference between reaching critical mass and achieving customer loyalty, or else there will continue to be a number of fatal new-company car crashes along the digital highway.

SCOTT MEDNICK

Former Chairman of Worldwide Xceed Group; Founder of Think New Ideas

Q **Ragas:** What advice do you have for a technology-focused organization on the topics of hitting critical mass and how critical mass once achieved can be translated into long-lasting customer loyalty?

A **Mednick:** Critical mass is obviously a very important part of any solid business. If you want to be the leader in a business, critical mass becomes very important. But I think the marketplace is now saying, "You're getting to critical mass, but at what cost?" This is Amazon.com's problem. Sooner or later, critics will say to Amazon, "What are we talking about here? You're not going to make money for five years? You lose hundreds of millions of dollars a quarter. What kind of a business is this?" If you gave me a hundred million dollars and I gave out ten dollars to every person I met to write me an e-mail, I would have more e-mails than anybody on earth! But that's not a business model. I would have spent an enormous amount of money to buy people's participation, but I haven't necessarily bought loyalty. Loyalty is a whole different thing, and I think people have confused critical mass with customer loyalty.

Q **Ragas:** So you're saying that the whole notion of reaching critical mass is pointless if a company hasn't achieved long-term customer loyalty. Otherwise, you've just created a very expensive revolving door!

A **Mednick:** I think that companies are just throwing numbers around. When you talk about critical mass, people say, "I'm getting 100,000 unique visitors to my Web site each month." Well, that's nice. But let's say you create Matt.com, and you call me up and say, "I'd like you to invest in my company. We had 50,000 unique visitors the first month, 100,000 visitors the second month, and 200,000 visitors the third month. Scott, we're doubling!" Well, what happens if I find out that the 50,000 that visited the first month didn't visit at all in the second month, and the 100,000 you had the second month weren't part of the traffic you received that third month? What you're really saying is that your company is good at getting people to only come once! That's not customer loyalty!

"I think people have confused critical mass with customer loyalty."

Honesty Is the Best Strategy

Now that you understand the difference between critical mass and customer loyalty, I thought it would be useful to explore ways a company can boost the customer-retention aspect of its business. This isn't hard to do if your organization is ready to take down the Plexiglas wall separating your employees and your customers and start being honest. Yes, honesty. Strip away the barrier that your sales people and marketing department hide behind as they craft flashy sales and marketing presentations full of the latest buzzwords that generally say very little. Tell the marketplace what your product or service really does and who your company really is!

As I pointed out in chapter five on brand building, digital customers can almost smell when a company is fibbing. The Internet is like one giant fact-checking machine just waiting for a company to stumble and spew out bogus product propaganda. Honesty is the best policy. Think about it for a moment. How refreshing does it feel when a salesperson directs you to another store where you can find a product you're looking for instead of trying to cram an alternate product down your throat! Tech companies that take this honest approach to customer relationships are reassuring customers that they see them as genuine friends and not simply as statistics.

A company that can make consumers think of it as being an honest group of people genuinely wanting to help is poised to see their customer loyalty rates skyrocket in future years. Organizations that choose not to follow this path of honesty will find themselves losing customers through the revolving door syndrome. As former AOL senior vice president Mark Walsh notes, tech companies that make a habit of lying to their customers will find the digital world to be as forgiving as a Biblical judge to a marketplace thief. Off with his hands! Critical mass can build companies, but critical mass without customer loyalty can turn on you and kill. It's that simple.

MARK WALSH

Chairman of VerticalNet;
Former Senior Vice President of America Online

Q **Ragas:** Many online and offline companies don't understand that capturing mind share, building critical mass, and achieving customer loyalty are all directly related to creating incredible trust in a company's customers. What advice do you have about trust and honesty?

A **Walsh:** The Internet rewards honesty and punishes duplicity. Prior to the Internet, sales were frequently made with lack of honesty and downright duplicity. A retailer on the East Coast, Sy Sims, owns a number of men's clothing stores. He runs a big radio ad campaign that says, "An educated consumer is our best customer." This ad says to the customer, if you know suits and you walk into a Sy Sims store, the salesperson won't have to sell you, because you'll know that this Ralph Lauren suit normally sells for $1,000, and it's only $300 at Sims. The trouble is, most businesses don't believe this! Most businesses want uneducated consumers so sales people can fill them with ideas that are friendly to the brand the salesperson is trying to sell.

Q **Ragas:** Yes. Unfortunately, a majority of companies have the philosophy that their job is to sell their product or service by fair means or foul, even if these one-time sales cripple their relationships with customers when they go to buy again!

"A digital customer who thinks you are a liar will use the bullhorn we call the Net to inform the world!"

A **Walsh:** I think what the Internet does magnificently is prove that Charles Darwin is right. I've been saying for years that the Internet accelerates time. Crappy businesses are discovered and shot down much faster today! On the positive side, good businesses are rewarded and grow. That's because the online buyer is able to compare all the different vendors. In this climate companies must be prepared to lose a sale by being honest with a customer. Gone are the days when companies constantly tried to flim-flam the customer that its products were the best! If you convince a customer that your products are best and they find out that you were bullshitting them, they can now use the Internet to bad mouth you with thousands of people instantly. Not only are you dead for lying, you have created a monster! A digital customer who thinks you are a liar will use the bullhorn we call the Net to inform the world! In today's marketplace dishonest companies lose. The good news is, honest companies win.

Listen to Your Customers

Even after you've come to grips with the realization that your company must be honest, your mission to enhance customer loyalty is still not finished. Sure, you've learned to walk the straight line of honesty and avoid marketing-speak with your product or service, but customers want to know that they are being heard when they speak. It is all too easy to ignore a customer complaint or suggestion. Somehow, e-mails and message board postings don't seem to have real faces behind them. They don't have the same impact as an irate customer screaming in the face of one of your salespeople. Nevertheless, the digital customer can raise more havoc in a flash of electrons than a flesh-and-blood customer ever will!

That's why companies that are masterful at maintaining high levels of customer services never fob off their customers with lip service and a pat on the back. They really listen and react. I'm not just talking about giving refunds or doing what it takes to satisfy a customer's order. Whether the customer is Joe Webhead in Idaho or a purchasing manager at IBM, companies that are experts at leveraging critical mass into long-term customer loyalty are constantly channeling their customers' input into the development of future products and services. It's always the customer who tells the company where it wants to go next, not the other way around. This is a simple concept, but there are still numerous engineering-driven tech companies that don't get it. They are about as flexible as Henry Ford, who once proclaimed that customers could have any color Model-T they liked, just as long as it was black!

Customer-driven technology organizations by their very nature are experts at translating initial customer mind share into long-term customer loyalty. Apple Computer has been able to maintain a rabid core following of customers for the Mac computer for over two decades, because Mac users feel they have real input into future Apple products. Smart companies aren't afraid to turn their customer relationships into a two-way conversation. They understand that if they consistently perform they will build great user loyalty for years to come. I think former IBM executive John Schwarz sums it up best when he says, "Listen to the customer and be flexible."

Make no mistake about it, discussions encourage trust, and trust helps build long-term customer loyalty. While incentive programs to reward frequent customers have become fashionable in the past few years, the fact remains that it is difficult to bribe a consumer or a business into long-term loyalty. Instead, use your existing critical mass to prove to your customers that future products and services will be built with their needs and desires in mind. The days of the all-knowing corporation are done. None of us hold all the answers. Trying to sail against the currents of consumer desire not only leads to fatal shipwrecks and drowned customers, it also destroys any customer loyalty you have established.

JOHN SCHWARZ

Chief Executive Officer of Reciprocal;
Former General Manager of IBM Solutions

Q **Ragas:** We have seen numerous examples of new companies in the tech marketplace that experienced incredible growth and quickly reached critical mass. Then, over time, their customer base melted away. What should companies do to maintain their existing customer mind share?

A **Schwarz:** The most important thing organizations must do for reaching and sustaining critical mass among their customer base is to surround themselves with industry experts who really understand the business of the customer. That is our most important success factor in persuading customers we are the best company for the job. The second thing I would point to as being very important is the willingness to go where the customer wants to

"We are absolutely willing to make the changes required. My advice: Listen to the customer. Be flexible."

go. In other words, we do not come into a meeting and say, "Here is a solution, Mr. Customer. Now buy it!" Instead, we go into every customer discussion and say, "What is your problem, Mr. Customer? How can we help you to solve it?" We have a solution in mind that is ready to go, but if the customer needs some changes or custom work done, we are absolutely willing to make the changes required. My advice: Listen to the customer. Be flexible.

CHAPTER 7

STRATEGIC PLANNING
IN THE DIGITAL DOMAIN

NEXT TIME YOU ARE AT THE BEACH, LOOK FOR A GROUP OF surfers. Watch how they paddle out into the waves with their boards and then wait patiently for the big waves to break. You will likely notice that a good surfer is constantly assessing which waves to paddle for and which waves to let break. A great surfer knows that exact instant ahead of time to catch the monster wave and ride it for all its worth. A great surfer also knows when to get off the wave before it drags him into shore to land on the jagged rocks!

Successful strategic planning in the technology industry is not really much different from the surfer and his assessment of the monster wave. Like the surfer checking the latest weather reports before entering the water, a smart company constantly works to gets its hands on the most up-to-date market intelligence on its competition and its industry.

At the same time, though, smart companies also rely on their own gut feelings and instincts, sometimes disregarding a truckload of data and heavy analysis. After all, there is something to be said about a grizzled surfer's ability to predict the weather more accurately than the meteorologists with all their millions of dollars worth of data and equipment!

In the digital business world of today, strategic planning has become compressed into a frenetic mix of art and science with few facts and dozens of assumptions. Those companies that can see the big waves forming before the rest of the pack does and then ride them into shore will continue to end up the big winners, while organizations too terrified to leave the comfy confines of a beach towel and oversized umbrella will slowly burn in the sun. Finding the right monster wave to ride is never easy, but as I will show you in this chapter, there are easy-to-follow steps that can substantially improve your chances of achieving long-term strategic planning success.

To begin this process, Artisan Digital Media president Nicholas van Dyk will expound on the difference between being a successful early player in a new market and a pioneer who ends up with arrows in his back. One of the recurring causes of failure of new, as well as established, companies, as we will find out from Tumbleweed's Jeff Smith, is that they often attempt to heap too many logs on the fire. In other words, companies must become insanely focused or they will perish. Even with a laser-beam focus, your company may still find its neat and tidy forecasts and projections coming to naught in the marketplace. That's why InfoSpace founder Naveen Jain will explain the importance of navigating by your gut as well as a spreadsheet.

Later in this chapter, with the help of Art Technology founder Joe Chung, we will delve deeper into the strategic planning process. Joe will stress the importance of "no-huddle" strategic planning that intertwines structure with flexibility.

Next, Vicinity chief Emerick Woods will share his tips and advice for identifying a company's true long-term competitors in the ever-changing dynamic of the marketplace. Finally, with assistance from Cobalt Group founder John Holt, I will explain a "fast follower" planning strategy that should allow your company to incorporate the innovations of newer industry players into your firm's existing products and services.

Learn to Walk Before You Run

The tech industry has a dangerous obsession with always wanting to be first. Rarely does a day go by that a venture capitalist, industry analyst, or executive at a digital company doesn't chatter on to all who will listen about the incredible importance of "first mover advantage." Instead of wanting to be the best, strategic planners in the tech sector have regrettably shifted their focus to wanting to be the first in a category. Clearly, there is a huge difference between these two goals. While being best focuses on delivering a superior value proposition, being first encourages companies to take gigantic leaps of faith on a regular basis.

While I am all for small and scrappy startups taking sizeable risks to help level the playing field, I don't believe companies should place bets on games the house hasn't even developed yet! In other words, betting big as a strategic planner is fine but don't gamble on undeveloped markets that have yet to show signs of growth. Sure, taking this approach might mean that your company doesn't end up as the next Microsoft or Oracle, but it does help insure that you won't end up as a sacrificial lamb on the "bleeding edge" either!

As much as you may constantly hear about the long-lasting value of the first mover advantage, there continues to be even more value in learning to walk first before you run into a new evolving market. Let other companies stumble around in the jungle fending off the wild animals and poisonous snakes! Learn from their mistakes. Being a first mover ended up being a huge advantage for an auction company like eBay, but first mover status did very little for pioneering online music seller CDNow or failed toys retailer eToys. These companies are now little more than memories in their respective categories.

Clearly, being first has some cachet, but I'd much rather be the best at anything I do. America Online wasn't the first interactive service, but it was better than the rest. Charles Schwab wasn't the first online broker, but it was better than the rest. Palm Inc. wasn't the first developer of handheld devices, but it was the best. This much is clear. In most cases, it is imperative that companies develop a focused strategy, even though this may mean they're not the absolutely first mover in a new market. Let other companies do the early missionary work for you. As Artisan's Nicholas van Dyk reminds us, pioneers are often the people face down in the dirt with arrows in their backs!

NICHOLAS VAN DYK

President of Artisan New Media, Executive Vice President of Artisan Entertainment

Q **Ragas:** What lessons and insights do you have for established businesses, as well as startups, that are attempting to anticipate and plan for the constant changes that occur in the online world?

A **van Dyk:** If you're starting from scratch with a company, you have to be aggressive and focused on taking risks, because risks will level the playing field for you. But if you're starting with existing assets and an offline business that has a unique value proposition to the customer, it's better to walk before you try to run! This way, you can oversee what happens and be ready to step in at some point. This strategic planning approach doesn't work, though, if you're selling the same thing that everyone else is selling with no real differentiation. Quite often, the pioneers are the people with their faces down in the dirt with arrows in their backs! In our case, we view the Web as an adjunct to our existing business, rather than a replacement for it. I came from the Walt Disney Company to Artisan about three years ago, and I was friends with many of the people who ran the pure-play Internet entertainment companies. I have always had great respect for these people, but I never believed in their underlying business models. My skeptical viewpoint has always been that there would be a huge bloodbath in this area and that maybe one or two companies would figure out how to be successful, but in the end the major movie studios will come in and take over. Because of this, we never felt like being huge pioneers in the content creation or e-commerce side of our business. My warning to others: Never forget the pioneers with the arrows in their backs!

> *"Quite often, the pioneers are the people with their faces down in the dirt with arrows in their backs!"*

Become Insanely Focused or Perish

High velocity and rapid change can do funny things to companies. Often, instead of placing just one log onto the fire and making sure that it burns, organizations end up dumping the whole woodpile into their fire. The more the merrier, I assume their thinking goes. What typically ensues is a huge fire that runs the risk of engulfing the entire company! Diversification is not always a bad thing, but when a company is trying to map its future, the last thing it needs is a zillion different ideas each screaming for attention and feeding. Focus works. It will force your company to rally around one idea. A dozen concepts can tear your company into warring factions.

Organizations faced with seemingly impossible odds whose members are all working towards the same goal can do amazing things. The fact is, one well-placed bet into a new market carries less risk than a strategic plan calling for multiple new products or services that stretch the ranks of your organization perilously thin. The success of search-engine company Google.com is a prime example of the value of maintaining focus and not trying to be all things to all people. When Stanford Ph.D. candidates Sergey Brin and Larry Page started Google in 1998, critics scoffed that a company focused purely on search would never develop into a successful business. Many industry analysts even suggested that the firm should eventually evolve into a full-fledged portal network like Yahoo or Lycos.

However, Google has managed to stay true to its original "strictly search" plan and today delivers arguably the best search experience on the Web. It consistently ranks as one of the Top 50 most-trafficked sites on the Web, is developing an incredibly loyal customer base, and is well on its way to profitability. One can almost guarantee that putting only one log onto the fire—in this case, search—was not always a comfortable feeling for Brin and Page, but their focus has paid off. The best strategic planners either become insanely focused or perish, as Tumbleweed's Jeff Smith points out.

JEFFREY SMITH

Founder, Chief Executive Officer, and President of
Tumbleweed Communications

Q **Ragas:** We seem to have entered into a period where a lot of young tech companies are driving blindly when it comes to strategic planning. Based on your own success, what advice do you have for these companies?

A **Smith:** Well, I believe that a company's failures are more interesting than its successes. I see so many companies that are so afraid of failing that they'll bury existing problems or they won't focus at all. They'll put fifteen logs on the fire, and they don't worry about one log that fails, because they assume that one of the others will succeed. The trouble is, these companies are ignoring the core challenge at hand, and most of them eventually fail. Companies must be willing to put just one log on the fire and make it burn. This approach is definitely scary, because you know that if you fail you really fail. It's also amazing what a company is capable of accomplishing once everyone understands what's make-or-break for the business.

> *"Companies must be willing to put just one log on the fire and make it burn."*

Q **Ragas:** Yes. By focusing on one specific near-term goal, an organization is forced to unify and rally around to solve that one particular problem. A make-or-break focus may not always feel comfortable, but it can move mountains, especially in scary situations.

A **Smith:** This approach to strategic planning is what Microsoft has done in spades. Microsoft took this exact approach with Windows 3.0. They basically said, We're going to take on IBM and OS/2, and it's make-or-break for our company. They then went out and told the financial analysts and the press that it was make-or-break. They told their employees, "This must succeed." Nothing was more successful in the history of computing than the release of Windows 3.0 and eventually Windows 95! The key to planning is the willingness to make this kind of bet and stand behind it. That's a hard thing for a company to do, because there isn't enough evidence to suggest the strategy will succeed. In fact, it's likely the evidence will suggest the strategy is even failing. If it were succeeding, you'd be at a later stage in your business. A company must really have the willingness to go out there and pursue that "one log" strategy and also to listen to where it may be failing.

Go with Your Gut, Not Your Spreadsheet

The movie *The Perfect Storm* made it clear that rarely does anything go according to plan when trying to navigate a boat through a vicious storm. Take away a ship's weather tracker, and the captain is left with only his instincts for navigation. Trust one's instincts, and the boat may live to sail the seas another day. Ignore them, and the entire crew may be swimming with the fishes sooner than they realize. The same goes for digital companies that get so caught up in the strategic planning process that they start listening more to the projections of market pundits and less to what their customers are telling them. Big mistake.

As I've pointed out throughout this book, ignoring the needs of your customers doesn't work. Customers are the ones who buy the new product or service that you produce. Don't be diverted by complex customer surveys and market research reports. Learn to take the "can't miss results" that pop up on these spreadsheets with a grain of salt. Sure, you might have just successfully hypothesized the next three to five years in your market, but you also might have created a bigger fantasy world than *Alice in Wonderland.*

Entrepreneurs who caught a monster wave by following their own instincts have built a number of the most successful companies of the past decade. Reams of market research didn't tell Dell Computer founder Michael Dell or Gateway founder Ted Waitt that consumers would flock to buy value-packed computers over the telephone and later the Internet. Deep in their guts these two men somehow just knew that this was what customers were secretly thirsting for! This is not to say that developing a detailed strategic plan for the future is a bad thing. Even though I'm sure Dell and Gateway both employ spreadsheet jockeys, I'm willing to bet it is the gut instincts of Waitt and Dell that still make both companies tick.

Strategic planning would be great if we could shrink the digital world down into a simple board game with pre-set rules and conditions, but this simply isn't the case. Especially in the digital domain, the evolution of a marketplace and a sector is impossible to successfully predict all of the time. After all, even with millions of dollars of sophisticated forecasting equipment, meteorologists still can't tell us when earthquakes are going to happen or exactly where hurricanes are going to hit. All we can plan for is how to react when catastrophe occurs. That's what InfoSpace founder Naveen Jain points out in our next interview. He says that the true key to strategic planning is simply to be a faster thinker and smarter reactor than your competition.

NAVEEN JAIN

Founder and Chairman of InfoSpace, Inc.; former Group Manager at Microsoft

Q **Ragas:** Even though a lot of the building and growing of a successful tech company comes down to flying by the seat of your pants, what insights do you have into the strategic planning process for a digital business?

A **Jain:** To be honest with you, the idea of planning is probably good for the people who aren't very smart. A lot of executives go into every meeting with a script for how everything should go in the meeting. It turns out that these people are the same ones who never come back with a signed deal. The reason for this is that nothing ever goes according to their original plan. The way you win in business is to always be the company or the person who is thinking faster than the other person. If you can think faster than the other person and analyze faster than the other person and always be two steps ahead of the other person, then you always win. You don't have to plan for it!

Q **Ragas:** While rarely anything in business ever goes according to plan, this "faster and smarter" element is one component to strategic planning that must be injected into the DNA of the entire organization. It can be the difference between life and death for a business when the original plan gets turned on its head.

A **Jain:** Yes. What I'm saying means that you have to be smart and very quick on your feet. Then you'll be able to make good decisions. In some sense, a lot of people go and say, "Okay. In this relationship, I'm going to put a spreadsheet together, and this is how this partnership should work." No. That kind of thinking is entirely wrong! Go with your gut and instead think to yourself, Does this deal feel right or does it not feel right? If it doesn't feel right, I don't care what spreadsheet you come up with, it's just not going to work! And if it feels good, I can definitely build a spreadsheet that will make everyone else feel good about it! I really believe that most long-term strategic planning is for the people at companies who cannot think fast enough on their feet. The world is moving so fast that by the time you finish writing a business plan it is already obsolete. In fact, I have never written a business plan in my life!

> *"The way you win in business is to always be the company or person who is thinking faster than the other person."*

"No-Huddle" Planning

Being a faster thinker and smarter reactor than your competition doesn't mean that your company will succeed when its original strategic plan is flipped upside down and turned inside out. Some organizations will always be better than others at taking a licking and keeping on ticking, but every digital company can take the necessary steps beforehand to better prepare for when the day of reckoning comes. Being faster and smarter doesn't mean your company will always choose the right path—just that you are smart enough to get out of the way before getting run over. It's always better to be a survivor than road kill. When your original strategic mission is drastically altered, you want to both survive and thrive!

A good way to understand successful strategic planning in the technology industry is to imagine a football team trailing by a touchdown with only two minutes left to play, and it has the ball. This is a smart team that refuses to panic. It switches to the "no-huddle" offense, with the quarterback calling the plays at the line of scrimmage as he surveys the defense. Savvy digital companies react the same way when they alter their near and long-term plans on the fly, but at the same time rely on their experience with their customers and suppliers to make well-informed decisions.

Sun Microsystems is an excellent example of a company that is a faster thinker, a smarter reactor, and also an expert at "no-huddle" planning. After being founded in 1982 as a manufacturer of UNIX-powered workstation computers, in the early nineties the company realized through talking to its customers the growing importance of Internet computing. Before most analysts began raving about that sector, the company quickly updated its servers for Web functions and aggressively moved into the network server market. While Sun still today derives a significant percentage of revenue from its workstation sales, the company is now the largest player worldwide in the UNIX-server market.

It's doubtful that Sun Microsystems CEO Scott McNealy would have guessed over eighteen years ago that network servers would ever evolve into the core growth driver of his business. However, by maintaining a flexible "no-huddle" approach to planning, the company has proven that it is not afraid to move into new markets based on a combination of gut instincts and past experience. By regularly challenging key assumptions that your company has made, you too should be able to better assess the current and future direction of your business and the sector market you are serving. As Art Technology Group's Joe Chung reminds us, smart companies must be willing to turn on a dime, but not all do so!

JOE CHUNG

Founder, Chairman, and
Chief Technology Officer of Art Technology Group

Q **Ragas:** So many young startups today seem to launch a new product or service without any regard for even near-term strategic planning. Is there any formula that companies can follow so they're not flying blind?

A **Chung:** What I find so fascinating about the Internet software business is that it has greatly compressed the time frame for change. Everything is changing very, very rapidly. Technology is changing. The market is changing. In business in general, there is no single formula that will work. You have to constantly adjust how you do things. The Internet is no different from any other industry— it's just faster. It highlights the need to not have a set pattern of attack. There really isn't a playbook, so we've gone through a lot of different ways that we think about strategic planning.

Q **Ragas:** Okay. Granted that there is no one set formula or playbook to follow in this business, I do believe there are a number of fundamental questions that businesses should periodically ask themselves to help plan for the future. This is sort of like going to get a checkup at the doctor's office.

A **Chung:** Periodically, your company should sit down and think about the last time you discussed the overall direction of your business and the market. You always have to make a number of fundamental assumptions and then go back and see if they are still true. This turns into a constant reassessment process. It's important to keep in mind, though, that many companies have stumbled because they are too flexible! These companies hop around so much that they never give any one business model a chance to mature. As a company, you have to be willing to turn on a dime, but you don't necessarily want to turn on a dime! So companies should always try to ferret out the irrational

> *"In business in general, there is no single formula that will work. You have to constantly adjust how you do things."*

pieces of their strategic assumptions and actively take part in a constant reassessment process.

Will the Real Competition Please Stand Up?

As part of strategic planning, successful digital companies must spend time learning who their long-term competitors are now and who might become the competition in the future. Especially in the technology business, looks can often be deceiving. A key supplier one day can evolve into a direct competitor the next, and a bitter age-old rival may eventually turn into one of your most trusted partners. The art of digital strategic planning is to mix hard facts and existing data with reasonable assumptions as you decide where your company's true competitors may lie in six months, a year, two years.

I'm willing to bet that if you had sat down with some traditional media executives in 1997 and asked them who they expected their major competitors to be on this new-fangled thing called the World Wide Web, they would either have scratched their heads or ticked off names of traditional media giants. Fledgling scrappy search engines like Yahoo, Altavista,

Lycos, and Magellan were hardly on their list at that time. By the same token, when Jerry Yang and David Filo were first developing Yahoo in a trailer at Stanford University, they weren't plotting to do battle one day against the likes of Time-Warner, Walt Disney, and News Corp.!

We all know this is what occurred. Search engines rapidly evolved into vast online media companies, and the biggest digital threat to traditional media companies has ended up not being each other but these once seemingly insignificant search-engine companies. This blending of such disparate worlds happens all the time in the tech sector. That's why it is important to constantly analyze where exactly your company sits in the value chain of a particular industry. You'll be better able to understand how complementary and adjacent companies may be trying to position themselves to move up to a more secure position in this chain.

Companies that regularly ignore this reanalysis of the value chain run the real risk of eventually being bushwhacked by their unseen competitors hiding somewhere in the brush, as Vicinity's Emerick Woods notes. Take a look at what happened to the Xerox Corporation. By the early seventies, Xerox was so convinced that its true long-term competitors would be large computer companies like IBM and Digital Equipment that it let Xerox-led innovations like the graphical user interface and Ethernet virtually walk right out the front door. Steve Jobs at Apple Computer and Bob Metcalfe at 3COM—not Xerox—ended up utilizing these groundbreaking technologies.

So be prepared. Don't become one of the victims of this creeping shift in the value chain of your particular industry. Become the experienced hunter instead. Do whatever it takes to stay on top of even the smallest tremors and movements in your marketplace at all times.

EMERICK WOODS

Chief Executive Officer and President of Vicinity; former Chief Executive Officer and President of TuneUp.com

Q **Ragas:** The tech marketplace today is so dynamic that keeping track of a company's competition is a full-time job in itself. What advice do you have for effectively tracking the competition?

A **Woods:** Keeping a close eye on the competition is very important for any tech company. But I think it is even more important to understand who your competition really is. Often, who a company may think is its competition is not. The reality of the tech industry is that it continues to evolve so quickly that a company's true competitors may wind up being companies that were originally in an adjacent or complementary industry. This shifting of competitors is particularly true in the New Economy where increasingly the name of the game is to "get big" really, really fast. This rush to reach critical mass results in a lot of consolidation taking place and means that some of the big corporations, who your company may not have originally even thought of as competitors, do suddenly wake up! Just look at the original search engine companies. Most of the companies that started out in the search-engine and portal business are no longer there, and there's been significant consolidation around a very small number of players. This is a lot like the old General Electric maxim. If you can't be number one or number two in your industry, then don't bother. I think that this maxim is going to be largely true in the New Economy arena as well. In most cases, there will be one, two, and certainly no more than three, dominant players in each market. So it's key that as a company you always know who your true competitors are!

> *"The reality of the tech industry is that it continues to evolve so quickly that a company's true competitors may wind up being companies that were originally in an adjacent or complementary industry."*

Follow the Nimble Innovators

If you have been successful at identifying your true future competitors while also practicing "no-huddle" strategic planning, your company will likely be presented periodically with a variety of ways to solidify and even enhance its market leadership. At market-leading or securely positioned companies, strategic planning doesn't necessarily require the organization to be the nimble innovator on the cutting edge of every new market opportunity. In fact, many of the most successful technology-focused companies have thrived by being fast followers, not nimble innovators. Think the cunning lion, not the fast cheetah.

By leveraging your company's core leadership position and absolute size in the marketplace, you should find it possible to rapidly incorporate and cherry-pick many of the best new innovations being pioneered by young startups in your sector. With proper timing, the established tech company is often able to move in quickly and swoop up the rewards, while the flock of young startups is forced to abandon their grueling pioneering work. Both Microsoft and Cisco Systems are masters at utilizing this approach to strategic planning as a platform to maintain their market dominance.

In the case of Microsoft, the company throughout its history has been adept at lurking in the background, patiently watching other companies blaze a new trail, and then turning on its fast-follower afterburners to rapidly seize the new market. Just ask fallen Microsoft rivals like Netscape, Lotus Development, and WordPerfect how effectively this strategy works. Cisco has also taken a very effective fast-follower approach to its Internet infrastructure business by making literally dozens of timely acquisitions of small and mid-sized innovative companies throughout its history.

Your company can effectively practice this fast-follower approach either through acquisitions or by modifying existing market innovations. The key lies in understanding the most relevant advancements in a market. Keep in mind the rewards are not in simply copying or acquiring every seemingly new good idea that comes down the pike. Copycats don't get nine lives! In fact, copying is likely to leave your organization feeling bloated, schizophrenic, and without focus. You need to be very selective with how you apply this fast-follower approach to strategic planning, as The Cobalt Group's John Holt notes in the next interview.

Finally, being a fast follower instead of a nimble innovator only works if your company's dominant market position has been achieved through a strong combination of critical mass and ensuing customer loyalty. If the loyalty piece of the equation is missing, all the modifying and copying of new market innovations in the world isn't going to help you or your firm. Build a solid foundation to your business first. Go back and reread the earlier chapters of this book. Then come back and use a mix of fast follower and no-huddle strategic planning, mixed with experience driven instincts, to maintain your new market position.

John Holt

Chief Executive Officer and
Founder of The Cobalt Group

Q **Ragas:** Based on your experience in growing The Cobalt Group, what lessons do you have for companies that are attempting to keep an eye on the competition while at the same time planning new growth initiatives for the future?

A **Holt:** With any Internet business, it's really difficult to know what's actually going on in the market because there are just so many bacteria growing. The digital world remains the most fertile and creative market I've seen in my lifetime. We've developed the confidence in our business to the point that we now don't have to be a nimble innovator. Sometimes, I believe a company can be very successful by being a fast follower. This approach is sort of like a big ship moving through the ocean creating a giant wake, where the wake actually acts as an attractant and brings smaller little boats into it. That's what those nimble little startups often become to large established companies!

Q **Ragas:** Right. A larger more established company that already has a strong foothold in its core market is often able to play the role of fast follower that profits off the innovations of the nimble innovator—if it can move fast enough.

A **Holt:** I also believe there's significant inherent cost savings in being a fast follower. Dell Computer is a fast follower. They took others' very good opportunities and executed better than the competition. Microsoft is also a very good fast follower. You have to be fast, though! This only works if your company pays attention to the market really well, because the opportunity for the fast follower is to see a new neat idea that will never get scale on its own, but that you can deploy quickly and win that market. We see this happen all the time in our own industry, where there are a number of very nice little companies that have some unique ideas that we can incorporate into our own business.

> *"We now don't have to be a nimble innovator. Sometimes, I believe a company can be very successful by being a fast follower."*

CHAPTER 8

HOW TO ATTRACT AND RETAIN TOP-NOTCH EMPLOYEES

AMERICAN INDUSTRIALISTS OF THE PAST LIKE ANDREW CARNEGIE, Cornelius Vanderbilt, and John D. Rockefeller would likely find the Information Age to be a cold and unfamiliar place. Since their time, a major shift has occurred in the economic landscape. In the New Economy, human capital has replaced industrial capital as the currency of the day. While fortunes are still being amassed today by controlling commodities like oil and steel, it is the companies that are finely tuned human-capital machines that have created the real wealth of the past fifty years. The collective brainpower of a company's workforce—not simply the combined output of its factories and machinery—is now the chief deciding factor in a company's success and failure.

In many respects, the importance of the intellectual power of a company's workforce has marked a complete shift in thinking from the American Industrial Revolution and the time when management totally controlled operations and workers. The drastic compression of time and the speed of innovation in today's tech sector do not allow companies to keep decision-making in the hands of a select few anymore. Command and control management for all intents and purposes is dead. Factory workers have turned in their work gloves and punch cards to make way for the return of skilled craftsmen who have a say in what the company does.

Successful technology-focused companies do in fact treat all of their employees like skilled craftsmen and truly value their workforce's input. They realize that demanding endless hours and monotonous work from their employees is the surest way to destroy their company. Factory thinking kills innovation, plain and simple. Nurture your human capital and mine it for fresh new ideas, or head to the nearest cemetery and purchase your business's burial plot right now!

Human capital, while arguably a technology company's most precious asset, walks out the door at the end of the day. Mistreat this incredible asset in any way, and in today's ultra-competitive marketplace there's a good chance it won't be coming back. In this chapter I will discuss the steps for hiring and retaining top-notch talent in your organization. To begin this process, I will share with you exactly how to start a human capital chain reaction, with assistance from Be Free's Gordon Hoffstein. Digex founder Doug Humphrey will then explain the importance of never hiring empire builders into your organization.

By following these two steps, you will have laid down a sturdy foundation to build upon for your next-tier hires, the employees I refer to as veteran athletes and gladiators. Junior Johnson of PurchasePro and Vicinity chief Emerick Woods will offer their firsthand experiences in making these hires. Of course, a company should not forget that effective human capital building is about much more than hiring for job skills, as I will explain with insights from FreeMarkets CEO Glenn Meakem. Finally, the last step in this process will be a checklist for finding out if you have in fact created what Flipside head Kenneth Cron refers to as a "hybrid vigor gumbo." Human capital is one pot that can never be stirred enough!

Great People Build Great Businesses

Ask the CEOs of successful tech companies for their secrets to success, and they'll probably tell you that smart people like to work with other smart people and that just average people attract and hire mediocre people. It's a fact of life. That's why the first ten, fifty, and even one hundred hires in any new company or newly formed division of a firm are incredibly important. They are truly the pillars that will help keep the roof from falling in on your company. Recruit pillars made of rotten wood instead of sturdy granite, and you deserve what you get!

The first step in the human-capital building process is to set sail with the brightest core team of employees possible. Without an original group of truly great people with "change-the-world" blood flowing through their veins, it won't matter that your company has the most whizbang technology in the marketplace or the biggest pile of venture capital the world has ever seen. You'll find a way to fail. Tainted or corrupted human capital almost always finds ways to tear even the greatest market opportunities apart, from the inside out.

As a young startup or small-established company suddenly experiencing an explosive growth curve, it's understandable to want to hire the first job applicants who come strolling through the door. When time is of the essence, every smiling face seems like a great prospect to throw a desktop computer in front of and quickly put to work. Stop. Reevaluate. Resist the urge. Be picky. Remember that great people attract other great people, and if you're trying to build a truly great business—which I assume that you are—then discipline and patience are the only ways to go.

I call it a human-capital chain reaction. If your first waves of hires are passionate, talented, smart people, then the human-capital building process will become increasingly easy as your company grows. Of course, it helps to have a truly unique and market-altering product or service to help stimulate this first important step in the process. Just imagine how many gifted programmers flocked to join Mark Andreessen and Jim Clark at Netscape Communications after word leaked out that the two were developing revolutionary technology for navigating the Web! As Be Free's Gordon Hoffstein notes, great people always find a way to make even a weak business work!

Gordon Hoffstein

Chairman and Chief Executive Officer of Be Free;
Founder of MicroAmerica Inc.

Q **Ragas:** You've built a number of tech companies throughout your career. Based on your experience, what have you found to be the most important foundation for building these companies and what lessons have you gained from these experiences?

A **Hoffstein:** One of the things that I've been asked for over twenty-five years now is what the secret formula is for business success. For me, it always comes down to the same thing, whether it is a business on the Web or off the Web, which is people. If you get good people, they'll figure out how to make a business work. A company can have weak technology, but good people will figure out a way to fix it. A company may not have a lot of money in the bank, but good people will figure out a way to get the idea funded. To make any business successful, start with

good, really dedicated people all working as a team toward
ing the same problems.

Q **Ragas:** Hiring really great people from day one almost starts
this powerful self-fulfilling prophesy. Your young company is destined to become a haven for lots of other smart people. Let's face
it. Smart people like to work with other smart people!

A **Hoffstein:** It wrecks companies that have great technology
and great financials when their people are fighting and not paying
attention to the customer. Again, it all
comes down to people. Anyone can have
a big building with lots of fancy computers and money in the bank, but it's a
company's people who always make the
difference. It all starts with having good
people and good leadership that can get
a company working together as a unit
to solve customer issues. Technology

> *"Anyone can have a big building with lots of fancy computers and money in the bank, but it's a company's people who always make the difference."*

doesn't always win. It all starts with great people and leadership.
The real magic to me to making a business really work is having
the right people with the right motivation!

Avoid Hiring Empire Builders

You must be careful to hire the right kind of smart people to
ensure your company of success in the human-capital arena.
I've seen two breeds of smart people in digital companies.
One is the individual who is not only passionate and smart,
but is a team player. This person honestly wants to see the
company succeed. The other type is the smart individual
who simply wants to build a fiefdom inside your company
and has a long list of hidden personal agendas and goals.
That's why it's so crucial that young companies don't allow

sting employees to bring aboard a boatload of past col-
eagues right at the beginning.

Since companies are typically most desperate for quali-
fied employees when they are first getting started, this is a
somewhat difficult hiring rule to follow. But it pays huge dividends down the line. Think about it. An empire builder is
the last thing any business needs when it is getting its engine
going. Your motto should be, Become unified or die. The
most talented software developer or marketing whiz in the
world isn't worth it if this person is going to cause dissension
in your ranks. As Digex founder Doug Humphrey bluntly
states, "There is only one empire and that is your company!"

Treat empire builders like skin cancer: Take all possible
preventive measures to avoid hiring them and cut them out
right away if they do appear. While it might seem easier to
scoop up a net full of fish instead of going for one fish at a
time with a rod and reel, the human-capital game comes
down to a business of hiring quality over quantity whenever
possible. A customer could care less how large your company's headcount is or how quickly you've ramped up your
organization! All your customers care about is that your
product or service is shipped on time and if your company
has delivered everything it promised. That's what matters.

DOUG HUMPHREY

Founder and Chairman of Cidera; Founder of Digex

Q **Ragas:** Tech startups as well as existing digital organizations
today are almost always in a frenzy to ramp up and rapidly hire
additional employees. What lessons do you have for companies in
the process of ramping the human-capital side of their operations?

A **Humphrey:** Here's a little lesson I've learned that I think is very
valuable. Let's say you have a nice little startup that is growing

quickly, and you need to hire a new head of information technology. At some point in time, you're going to hire someone who is going to try and walk in and create their own little empire. You have to be careful about people like this. That's not what you hired them to do. You probably didn't go to them and say, "We're stupid and would like to start from scratch!" That's probably not what your company needs, but unfortunately a lot of startups try it. When hiring people, you need to make clear you are hiring them to add to your existing team and not to come in and clean out the people who are there!

Q **Ragas:** In other words, companies need to be extremely careful to hire executives who are team builders, not fiefdom creators. Otherwise, you run the risk of building a fractious organization with a variety of different goals and hidden agendas always floating around.

A **Humphrey:** You can create a lot of strife and internal dissent when someone comes in from the outside with an agenda. When you hire a new executive, you should have a rule that says they can bring no more than one or maybe two people with them that they have worked with previously. You don't want them to immediately start bringing in everyone from their last job. As someone once said to me, I don't mind having an old boys' network, but why do we have to have someone else's old boys' network? The real issue is that empire builders need to be taken behind the dumpster and shot! They do nothing but damage a company. There is one empire and that is the company. If you have someone in your company building their own empire, then they are making decisions not with the best interests of the company in mind, but their own. Don't let that happen!

> *"The real issue is that empire builders need to be taken behind the dumpster and shot! They do nothing but damage a company."*

Hire Great Athletes Who Have Run This Race Before

Now that we have learned to avoid empire builders at all costs, it is important to focus on what type of great people growing companies should hire. The next step in the human-capital building process is to recruit into your organization employees that have already run the startup race before. In other words, hire veteran athletes who already understand the challenges that come with operating in a fluid work environment without a clear chain of command for an extended period of time. Since any emerging marketplace is already chock full of minefields, you should at least try to begin the battle with a core team that has been in combat before.

By bringing aboard these veteran athletes, not only will your organization cut down drastically on the training aspects of the learning curve for operating in a startup environment, but the company will also gain valuable leadership expertise. Bringing aboard a mix of young rookies fresh out of school is fine, but in the race to scale and rapidly capture a market, the more experienced hands you have on deck the better. After all, no successful business grows without making some mistakes. Don't you want to have your company heavily fortified with veteran startup workers when someone pulls a "grenade pin" by accident in your formative days? Yep. I thought so.

Many of the Internet's earliest and most successful companies clearly took this "hire veteran-athletes" strategy to heart. While Yahoo, Lycos, and Excite were all founded by young hard-charging entrepreneurs, all three companies were quick to bring veteran leadership into their organizations very early in their existences. While it's hard to gauge what long-term effect these hiring decisions had on the outcome of each company, one thing I do know is that even amidst a brutal shakeout among the portal industry, these companies remain among the Web's ten most trafficked online properties today.

Let's face it. In the race to lower your company's learning curve, startup veterans already know how to win; no one has to sit them down in seemingly a zillion different pricey training seminars and show them. Raw talent may be able to match experience or even surpass it for a while, but sheer enthusiasm and drive aren't what win markets long term. In fact, having too much of either is a good way to ensure a false start before your new product or service even launches. Perhaps Vicinity's Emerick Woods summed it up best when he calmly told me, "Find great athletes who have already run this race before!"

EMERICK WOODS

Chief Executive Officer and President of Vicinity; former Chief Executive Officer and President of TuneUp.com

Q **Ragas:** Rapidly growing a technology-focused company is never easy. Adding so many new employees in such a compressed time frame almost always creates room for error. So what are some ways that companies can significantly lower the risk of shooting blanks in the human-capital arena?

A **Woods:** One thing that is really constant in the technology industry is change. A lot of this change a company can never really figure out beforehand other than to go out and actually get right in the middle of it. Having related experience beforehand is a huge advantage. In most cases, there are no real signposts on this road of change! I will also say that one of the keys to managing in a hyper-growth environment is to hire employees who have operated in an environment of tremendous change before. People often talk about the athlete model and building a company's organization by going out and trying to acquire really good athletes. But I think the real key is to hire a really great athlete who has already run the race before. Ultimately, what you want is an employee in your company who immediately says, "I've seen this

"I think the real key is to hire a really great athlete who has already run the race before."

play before or I've run this race before." Yes, some of the challenges in this new race may be different. Maybe working in a fast growing digital business instead of a rapidly growing offline company is a little bit like running on a tartan track instead of a gravel track, but by and large, these people already know what they need to do!

Hire Gladiators, Not Big Thinkers

Once you have sprinkled all departments of your organization with solid veteran athletes, the next step in the human-capital building process is to surround these athletes with proven winners. When I say "winners," I don't necessarily mean individuals who have worked in a technology-focused enterprise before. I'm talking about people who are competitive by nature and hate to lose at anything they do. Call them whatever you like— fighters, scrappers, gladiators, or warriors—but these individuals are the true lifeblood of any successful digital company, as PurchasePro's Junior Johnson points out in the next interview.

Proven winners don't mind putting on their flack jackets and helmets when the going gets tough. Unfortunately, many technology companies today focus so intently on hiring employees either directly out of school or from their industry that they let many unorthodox proven winners fall through the cracks. Don't let this happen in your own business. Invest the time to recruit and train proven winners for lower level and mid range positions in your organization. The end result will be a workforce that is much more loyal to your company than the typical fly-by-night stock option crowd.

Although vision is nice, execution is everything. At the end of the day it is the gladiators—not the ivory tower thinkers—who really make a company hum. Look at America Online. Here is a company with a handful of big thinkers and literally thousands of "grind it out" customer service and technical support warriors who are passionate about executing on the company's vision. While AOL founder Steve Case had the original vision for an online service back in 1985, it was his team of unheralded operational, technical, and marketing gladiators in the company's earliest days who put their noses to the grindstone and never broke under repeated attacks from much larger rivals like Prodigy and CompuServe.

CHARLES JOHNSON JR.

Founder, Chairman, and
Chief Executive Officer of PurchasePro.com

Q **Ragas:** You've been a serial entrepreneur for your entire life. As you have built your various businesses and rapidly ramped them up with new employees, what have you found to be the most important traits and skills to look for in a new hire?

A **Johnson:** I think in this world it's essential for companies to hire competitive people who are interested in winning. Especially in the technology business, so many people just focus on the resumes of potential employees, what schools they attended, and what consulting company they worked for previously. They forget that, at the end of the day, you need winners. Companies should find people who have been successful and winners in other areas of their lives but maybe underachieved in business because they didn't have the right leadership or their skills weren't used properly. Perhaps the hardest thing, though, is to take these people and let them know they are the real policymakers and policy changers now—not simply policy followers. If I had to say one thing about human capital, it is, Always hire competitive people.

Q **Ragas:** So what you're saying is that in many cases you'd much rather hire the trainable proven winner than the individual who is clearly smart but may not be committed to sticking things out during a rough patch. Companies need employees in this business who don't mind staying down and dirty in the trenches.

A **Johnson:** Everyone assumes you are going to try to hire smart people, but I'd much rather hire smart and competitive people. What happened when the stock market made its adjustments was that competitive people didn't look back! They know at the end of the day where they're going to end up: on top. It's like if you have a good football team that's down ten points. They're not worried about losing; they're planning how they're going to win! We have a saying here: Money follows success; success does not follow money. The other saying that has always been true for me is, "Those that do that which is for least always do that which is most." If you've got someone that does all the little things from a competitive standpoint, you'll see that little numbers turn into big numbers. If you've got someone that focuses on the little things, then the big things always happen. Most organizations have all these people with these big, thirty-thousand-foot views. That's great, but at the end of the day, we work on the ground. That other visionary stuff is great, but in reality we work on the ground!

> *"Everyone assumes you are going to try to hire smart people, but I'd much rather hire smart and competitive people."*

Hire for Character Traits, Values, and Job Skills

Not every veteran athlete or proven winner is created equal. Individuals have their own sets of unique core values and

character traits—some good, some bad. Success an
can mean vastly different things to different people. Wg
in mind, we'll look at the next step in the human-capital b
ing process. This is to make sure that your organization shan
the same values as the employees you are hiring.

It makes sense that if your goal is to build a company that
is honest and respectful to its customers, your new hires shoul
all share your values. After all, it is a company's employees—
not a lofty mission statement written by the board of directors—
that shapes the culture of the organization. Don't think for a
second that customers can't see right through a com-pany's
flashy sales brochure into the shifty eyes of a dishonest salesperson trying to sell your product or service.

Don't allow your human resources department to fall into
the trap of filling positions solely on the basis of finding applicants with matching job skills. These skills really mean very little if the individuals with them carry lots of baggage in the
character traits department. Hiring out-of-character applicants
is a surefire way to wreck your company. Think of it this way:
Job skills can be developed and refined, whereas individuals'
core values rarely change. There are exceptions to this rule,
but why try to swim against the tide when there undoubtedly
are job seekers out there who share your core values?

Remember, you are building an enduring team with a
common goal and one core set of values, not a loose federa-
tion of fractious workers all with their own codes of ethics.
There must be harmony in your ranks, as well as a company-
wide vision with corresponding values that your entire organization can rally around and communicate to the public.
That's why leading application-server software company
Citrix Systems goes as far as having all potential mid-level
hires spend an entire day at the company being interviewed
by existing employees throughout the organization, before
they make a hiring decision.

he end result of Citrix's multi-level hiring process is a
pany with a feeling of increased team unity and an
nization that is constantly double, triple, and even
druple checking itself to make sure that it continues to
ld true to its core values. That's why I'm a firm believer in
e importance of worrying less about potential employees'
skill sets and more about who they really are as people. You
can take this following statement to the bank. Great people
build great companies, and a business can never have too
many honest and hard-working team members, as
FreeMarket's Glen Meakem reminds us.

GLEN MEAKEM

Founder, Chairman, and
Chief Executive Officer of FreeMarkets

Q **Ragas:** Young companies almost always focus their initial attention on securing venture capital and striking early alliances, but it
seems that human capital, arguably the most crucial component of
any digital business, usually gets ignored in the startup shuffle.

A **Meakem:** Yes. The biggest challenge by far in any business is
people. You have to hire really great, great people. You have to hire
not only for job skills but also strong character traits and values. If
you want an honest company, you need to hire honest people. I've
found myself frequently in a position where I've hired a person with
the right character traits and values, but they might not have the
right set of skills for the job that I originally hired them for. I've found
that if they are hard-working and have the right character, I can usually find a role that fits them. An employee may have joined your
company thinking that they were a salesperson, but after a few
months you realize they would fit better as a recruiter. We have some
great examples of people who have actually changed whole areas
of responsibility and flourished in their new roles.

Q **Ragas:** There are still many companies, though, that end up hiring the wrong person for a position, simply because they didn't focus enough on human-capital development in the first place. They were just trying to rapidly put more warm bodies in cubicles.

A **Meakem:** People put a lot of focus on marketing, sales, and technology, but typically neglect to place a huge focus on the people function. We don't even call this area human resources in our company. We call it people development. Recruiting, performance evaluation, organization design, and compensation are the keys to people development. Companies must get the employee stock option program, employee salaries, and bonuses correct from day one. Senior management has to give serious attention to those topics. If people aren't being rewarded, compensated, and regularly evaluated, you're not going to be successful!

> *"You have to hire not only for job skills, but also strong character traits and values. If you want an honest company, you need to hire honest people."*

Develop the Right Blend of People

Assuming you've followed all of the human-capital building steps until this point, it's now time to check the people pulse of your organization. If you've successfully worked through the first five steps of this process while growing your workforce, your company should now have created what Flipside's Ken Cron calls, "hybrid vigor gumbo." In other words, your business should now boast a diverse blend of male and female employees from a wide variety of backgrounds, ages, and nationalities. In addition, your business should now be filled with a sturdy mix of veteran athletes and proven winners, employees who eat, sleep, and breathe your company's core values and beliefs.

Capturing this hybrid vigor within an organization is the real secret to long-term employee retention. Boosting compensation and increasing paid vacation days are nice side benefits, but what really motivates and keeps most employees is an ongoing feeling of belonging and sense of achievement. If all they cared about was getting rich, any really smart person today could go to work for a dozen different companies. Your employees must believe they are not just another number or face in the crowd, but unique individuals making unique contributions to a product or service that might just make the world a better place.

Pundits can criticize Microsoft all they want, but the fact of the matter is that even twenty-five years after being founded, almost all Microsoft employees still believe they can actually change the world and that Microsoft is the best place to accomplish this. Bill Gates and Steve Ballmer may eternally have the government breathing down their necks, but they have managed never to lose their hybrid vigor gumbo. If human capital is the core foundation to any successful company today, then hybrid vigor is clearly the special mortar that holds the building blocks together through every conceivable disaster.

KENNETH CRON

Chief Executive Officer of Flipside, Inc.;
former President of Publishing of CMP Media

Q **Ragas:** The importance of building the right mix of employees in an organization may be more crucial today than ever before, as we move further into a digital world. What lessons do you have for companies hoping to create the perfect human capital gumbo?

A **Cron:** First of all, industrial capital has largely been commoditized. So success or failure for companies today is much more about getting into the right markets and being nimble in these markets. This all comes down to people. What we try to do at Uproar is to combine seasoned and talented people. It really takes a diverse group to create the hybrid vigor that will carry a company forward. You need to blend seasoned managers with the twenty-three-year-olds. This younger group has grown up with the Internet and "gets it." But, if you have a company that is all from the same generation, you are setting yourself up for obsolescence! Companies should have a blended group. I believe these young people should have positions at "close to the road" levels, as well as high levels in the organization. I think this is also true for some of the more seasoned people, and by this I don't mean just age. You need this at the top as well. For example, our head of products and technology is only twenty-something, and his team is very young also. Yet our sales and marketing head worked with me at CMP Media and is forty-five years old or so. His two lieutenants, though, are in their mid twenties. It's this blending that is just so important!

"If you can mix and match—in gender, age, and culture—then you've created the hybrid vigor that every company needs!"

Q **Ragas:** Therefore, companies must find ways to intertwine these different generational groups throughout the various layers and levels of their organization. When done properly, the end result is a powerful human-capital-based system of "checks and balances" within the business.

A **Cron:** Yes. This same blending is also important with gender. Having a mix of gender at all levels is key and important to a company's success so you don't create the old boys' club or the old girls' club. I think neither one is a formula for success. Culturally you need to have this type of mix as well. We bought a company in Israel. We were founded in Budapest, Hungary. We have very strong relationships in both India and Asia in terms of our employee base. We have a very diverse work group culturally. I think this is key, because the world is coming closer together, and ideas are becoming more transparent across borders. It is absolutely key that these cultural differences get exemplified. When you do this, you see this enthusiasm become the nucleus for where the world is going to go and where your company is going to go! If you can mix and match as I've described at all levels of your company—in gender, age, and culture—then you've created the hybrid vigor that every company needs!

CHAPTER 9

THE ART OF BUILDING A LONG-LASTING E-ORGANIZATION

WHILE THE MOST IMPRESSIVE SHEPHERDS OF HYPER-GROWTH organizations in the last decade are without doubt Andy Grove at Intel and Bill Gates at Microsoft, sometimes it is easier to look in the history books for management models than in the corporate boardroom. Let's use as our historical example the most phenomenal hyper-growth managers of the past two centuries, the great patriots of the American Revolutionary War.

Just like a typical startup company today, the Founding Fathers began their quest for freedom as a handful of men in one room. They were cash strapped like many young companies, with only sheer gumption, unlimited passion, and some loans and voluntary contributions to keep them going. Anyone taking bets on the eventual winner of this war back then would have given odds of at least a million to one! In the face of seemingly dismal prospects, the Founding Fathers persevered and were able to turn thousands of untrained farmers and artisans into an army that eventually crushed the seemingly invincible British forces.

The plight of a young technology-focused business is really not very different from that of the Founding Fathers. Competition today isn't the redcoats, but every hyper-growth business is forced to deal with rapid-fire decision making and drastic ramping up of their organization as they try to fend off external threats in the marketplace. For many companies, this seems like an impossible task to accomplish all at once, but as you will see in this chapter, there is a series of clear steps to hyper-growth management that any rapidly growing business can follow to mold itself into a successful, long-lasting organization.

First and foremost, hyper-growth management can never be successful unless all members of the organization become strident believers in the long-term goals of the business. To help us do this, BlueLight's Mark Goldstein will offer his insights on how to make "change the world" flavored Kool-Aid. Next, Chris MacAskill of MightyWords will expand on my own belief that inflated false expectations have been instrumental in destroying many a promising company. After reviewing how to avoid creating false expectations in your firm, you will then learn from K. B. Chandrasekhar why every rapidly growing company should bring aboard an experienced leader at a certain point in the growth cycle.

Along with the rapid velocity of change that comes with competing in the Next Economy, I will outline with iBeam's Peter Desnoes why companies that try to make the absolute best decisions will fail. A mentality of not making the wrong decision must reign supreme. Next, INTMedia Corp. founder Alan Meckler will point out the importance of a firm's foot soldiers always having confidence in their organization's senior management. Lose the foot soldiers' confidence and you will undoubtedly lose the war. As a final step in this process, Junior Johnson of PurchasePro and I will show why organizations must adopt the mentality that believes expanding and contracting their company can be a good thing.

Preach and Live the Hyper-Growth Religion

The foundation of hyper-growth management begins with the transformation of a company's workforce into a fervent community of strong believers. You must preach the hyper-growth religion to your troops and then live it. It may sound ridiculous, but employees of the most successful tech companies are ready not only to work for four days straight without sleep, but to walk on hot coals to make their company succeed!

As surprising as it may sound, the early days of management at almost any technology-focused business are less about strategic thinking and more about developing a visionary creed that the entire organization can follow and live by. Next time you are flipping through the television channels, stop and watch a Sunday morning reverend delivering his fire and brimstone sermon. Become that reverend inside your own company. Preach the theme, "We can change the world together" and transform your company's doubters into believers. You have no other choice. After all, if your workforce doesn't believe, then I can assure you that your prospective customers, suppliers, and investors won't, either!

I can't stress enough how absolutely crucial it is that your own employees believe, from day one, that your company is going to go out and change the world. They must wholly embrace your vision for the future. Naturally, if you do have a unique and superior product or service, instilling this "change-the-world" mentality into your workforce is very doable. When all is said and done, human beings inherently want to be able to look into someone's eyes and believe that something "bigger and better" is out there.

Look around at some of today's most successful digital companies, and you'll find that almost all of them have their own almost cultlike organizational cultures. Furthermore, many employees of these companies actually believe they are out to change the world and that they were each specially selected for this higher mission. This type of behavior might sound foreign to startup outsiders, but it is hard to imagine a fledgling tech company surviving the hardships of hyper-growth by doing things any other way. As BlueLight.com's Mark Goldstein points out, the key to keeping employees motivated and passionate is to create a "change-the-world environment" that really smart people can't resist being part of.

MARK GOLDSTEIN

President and Chief Executive Officer of BlueLight.com; former Vice President of Inktomi

Q **Ragas:** One of the biggest obstacles a startup faces is that, amidst all of the commotion that comes with hyper-growth, it can lose its focus, leaving many of its workers feeling disenfranchised. What advice do you have for keeping your employees satisfied and focused?

A **Goldstein:** What it really takes to keep employees interested and motivated is to build a work environment that people actually want to be part of! For me, the key to successfully building this environment goes back to my experience with Apple Computer in the early eighties. Apple founder Steve Jobs did this really well. In my mind, he's going to go down as the ultimate entrepreneur of Silicon Valley, perhaps even more so than the Hewlett-Packard founders, because he talked to a different generation. Basically, what Steve Jobs was all about was changing the world and getting everyone else to believe this also. He said to everyone, "We can get out there and really change things! Drink my special Kool-Aid, and we'll go out there and change the world." That kind of enthusiasm and passion really infected folks. It worked! I think that type of change-the-world thinking is still very much what's going on within most startup companies today. Every new company still wants to go out into the market and become the best and the greatest. So companies must convince their employees that they are going to go out there and change this world—whatever "this world" might be—if they want to be successful!

> *"What it really takes to keep employees interested and motivated is to build a work environment that people actually want to be part of!"*

Don't Become a Victim of False Expectations

Once you have helped nurture a change-the-world culture in your organization, it is important to realize how extremely fragile your "company religion" is. It is young and untested. Employees will only remain strident believers in your business as long as they can periodically see, touch, and feel new signs in the marketplace that reinforce their beliefs. This means that simply pumping your company up with hot air about wonderful pending alliances and record-breaking sales forecasts won't do the trick if it isn't the truth! There must be more than just the flashing lights of Oz behind the giant curtain that conceals your business.

One of the many reasons for the failures of dot-com companies is that they became victims of inflated false expectations. Setting high but attainable performance expectations is one thing for a young company, but setting ludicrous goals that even a team of superhuman people couldn't reach is another! After all, even a young child that is told she will win a prize if she cleans her room, quickly loses interest in this task if the parent doesn't follow through and reward her. Employees are no different. They must periodically see rewards—such as new customer wins and on-time product launches—to confirm in their minds that progress really is being made on their mission to change the world.

The solution to not becoming a victim of inflated false expectations is to set, and then convey, realistic growth targets and attainable goals for your entire organization. While this sounds simple, it isn't. As an entrepreneur or company manager, you may want to deal solely with fantasyland goals and pie-in-the-sky projections that sound impressive (at least on the surface) to reporters, employees, and investors. While this behavior is bad enough, the same companies that proclaim these "pie-in-the-sky" goals to others often end up believing this nonsense themselves. Your company might as well hire a bankruptcy attorney if this starts to happen.

To prevent this pie-in-the-sky syndrome from invading your own company, let me quickly remind you that many of today's most successful and long-lasting digital companies—ranging from Hewlett-Packard and IBM to Microsoft and Intel—didn't try or promise to take over the tech sector in only one week. They didn't try to turn into a multi-billion-dollar company in one Sunday afternoon, and they certainly didn't plan to have an initial public offering after being in business only two years. Let's face it: Changing the world takes time. Be patient. Your day will come. As MightyWords.com chief Chris MacAskill notes, by stating realistic goals, your company can drastically improve its chances of surviving the harsh winter.

CHRIS MACASKILL

Founder of FatBrain.com;
Chief Executive Officer of MightyWords.com

Q **Ragas:** Hyper-growth management is a lot like trying to manage the development of the first rocket to the moon. With so much to do, it's easy for a company to implode under the sheer weight of the goal at hand. Do you have any suggestions on steps companies can take to make sure they don't explode on the launch pad?

A **MacAskill:** First of all, I don't believe that you really can build a solid organization if you have to build it at lightning speed. I think of hyper-growth management as taking care of a group of young trees that grow really fast. You give them too much nitrogen and they grow really fast, but when winter comes, a lot of the limbs break off. The companies we all admire so much, like Sun, Cisco, Dell, and Hewlett-Packard, have all been able to post respectable and steady growth year after year. These companies all set realistic expectations about how much they could grow. They didn't try to triple or quadruple sales in only a year. Think about how many companies we've seen recently that took off like weeds right out of the starting gate but have now failed!

Q **Ragas:** Yes. I definitely can't count that high! What you're suggesting then is that companies set sensible and realistic growth goals and profitability targets to meet each quarter, instead of pie-in-the-sky projections that leave their businesses set up for failure from day one!

A **MacAskill:** Right. I heard Netscape and Silicon Graphics co-founder Jim Clark speak recently at an event where the audience asked him what his greatest success ever was in business. He said founding Netscape. Then someone asked him why Netscape decided to compete in the Web-browser business in which it would ultimately lose, instead of trying to become a portal like Yahoo. Clark said that, in retrospect, while it is dead obvious today that

"I think of hyper-growth management as taking care of a group of young trees that grow really fast."

they should have become a portal, they were just growing so fast. Netscape probably felt like they were getting sucked up into the center of a tornado! Which reinforces my point. Many of the technology companies that initially grew at ultra warp speeds like Amazon.com are now in trouble. Now

that winter has set in, some of their branches are dying. I'm sure the trees will still stand, but I'm not sure what kind of wood is going to fall off when the wind starts blowing!

Turn Over the Reins to a Jockey Who Knows How to Win the Race

Even companies that do ultimately survive the harsh winter by setting realistic expectations reach a point in their growth cycle when they typically need a boost to reach the next level. Otherwise, they run the risk of plateauing before they reach their ultimate potential. One of the real keys to successful hyper-growth management is for the company's founders and existing management team to identify when it is time to pass the baton to a more experienced runner—and then do so.

Blockbuster tech successes like eBay, Yahoo, America Online, Exodus Communications, and Akamai Technologies were all quick to realize early on that once their business models had been proven in the market it was time to recruit an experienced captain to steer the ship. It is hard to dispute that the hiring of former Hasbro executive Meg Whitman to run eBay was the smartest and most important decision eBay founder Pierre Omidyar ever made. The same goes for

Yahoo founders David Filo and Jerry Yang's very early hiring of Tim Koogle, an established tech industry veteran, as CEO of Yahoo way back in 1995.

Clearly, the skill sets required to see a compelling market opportunity and start a company, as opposed to actually growing and leading an increasingly complex organization, couldn't be more different! That's why, although there have been some high-profile exceptions like Bernie Ebbers of WorldCom and Larry Ellison at Oracle, most successful technology-focused organizations today are run by professional managers and not the companies' founders. The compression of time and velocity of change in the Next Economy simply does not allow most entrepreneurs to morph from one role into the other.

That's why Exodus founder K. B. Chandrasekhar implores entrepreneurs to stop "tinkering around" once their company's business model has been proven and to step to the sidelines. In other words, the next step in the hyper-growth management process is to turn the reins of the business over to a jockey who already knows how to win the race and then let that person move the company forward.

K. B. CHANDRASEKHAR

Chief Executive Officer and Chairman of Jamcracker Inc.; Founder of Exodus Communications

Q **Ragas:** You took Exodus from being a mere pipsqueak into the largest Web-hosting and services company on the planet. What is the key to successfully managing the ramping up of a hyper-growth business so it doesn't wear down or even get torn to pieces in the process?

A **Chandrasekhar:** What immediately comes to my mind is the absolute importance of bringing experienced managers into a business very early on. In our case, we hired Ellen Hancock, a former IBM executive, to be the CEO of Exodus Communications. The thing you have to realize as an entrepreneur as your business rapidly grows is that your purpose is no longer about "tinkering" here and there. It is fundamentally about achieving broader scale execution. This means that you must get the people who have "been there, done that" and know how to get from one point to the next. Tinkering is what you do when you are still trying to prove the business model. Once the business model is

"Entrepreneurs really must evaluate themselves to see what it is they enjoy doing the most and what they are really good at."

tested and ready for the mass market, don't tinker with it. That's when you need to bring in experienced management like AOL founder Steve Case did by recruiting an experienced executive in Bob Pittman. We did it at Exodus by hiring Ellen Hancock. When investors come to you, they come to you because they think you know how to build something, but not all by yourself. They do expect that you know how to get the best horse to win the race. This is not about ego. Entrepreneurs really must evaluate themselves to see what it is they enjoy doing the most and what they are really good at. If you allow yourself to get confused between the two, you can easily end up with a disaster on your hands!

The "Absolute Best" Decisions Take Too Much Time

One important component of bringing in an experienced executive to lead a rapidly growing organization is that the move forces the company to admit to itself that it doesn't always have the best answer to any given problem. If it did, it wouldn't have ventured outside its corporate walls to recruit a jockey who already knows how to win the hyper-growth race. This realization is crucial, because the velocity of change occurring in the Next Economy and the compression of time taking place simply does not allow for always making the absolute best decision. Until a company realizes this, it is driving at night with the headlights off.

In a traditional business environment, there typically is time to conduct research and detailed due diligence before making major decisions about increases in production, marketing expenditures, or dissolving a pending or existing alliance. In the tech business, everything happens in fast-forward mode. Tech companies that use up time weighing their options and always searching for the absolute best decision often find themselves left behind. For the most part, the Next Economy is about acting and reacting once the ball has been set in motion, only pausing to decide when the ball will stop moving or how it was even set in motion in the first place.

The real key to decision making in a hyper-growth environment is to eliminate all the options that could result in a fatal car crash for the company and then quickly make a decision from the remaining choices. Instead of always trying to make the absolute best decision, a hyper-growth business learns to focus its efforts on not making the wrong decision. It's a lot like how someone reacts if they are under fire in combat. Instead of waiting to take a perfect shot, a soldier is much more likely to target his enemy as quickly as possible and then fire. As iBeam's Peter Desnoes reminds us, adjustments to a non-fatal decision can always be made later.

PETER DESNOES

Chief Executive Officer and President of iBeam Broadcasting; former Chief Executive Officer of Burnham Broadcasting

Q **Ragas:** You've now run two very substantial traditional and technology-focused organizations. What are some of the key lessons you've learned about hyper-growth management in the Next Economy that you can share with us?

A **Desnoes:** I had a revelation last year that really led to a number of management changes in our organization. We originally had a culture that tried to make sure we always made the right decision. I came from a culture in television at ABC and with my own company where we always tried to make the right decisions. However, this kind of thinking just doesn't work in the New Economy! Trying to always make the absolute best decision in the New Economy is just too high a threshold. You have to move too fast in this business! Therefore, companies must adopt a culture where they don't make the wrong

"Trying to always make the absolute best decision in the New Economy is just too high a threshold."

decision. Now that may sound like the same thing, but it is really very different. Making the wrong decision is the same thing as making a dumb or ill-informed choice. A New Economy company's goal is to make sure it doesn't make a decision that will truly cripple it down the road.

Q **Ragas:** Speed of decision making is definitely of the essence in the Next Economy. As you pointed out, the days of making the absolutely perfect decision are done. There's just no time for that! Companies must learn to act quickly and decisively. The days of calling a dozen meetings and conducting detailed due diligence before making a decision are history!

A **Desnoes:** As an example, let's say that there are ten logical choices to a decision. Five of the choices are good and five of the choices are bad. I believe that in the New Economy a company must first eliminate the five bad choices. If a company has narrowed its list down to the five remaining good choices, it should then just pick one of them. Don't spend time trying to figure out which one is the best out of the remainder! Trying to always pick the absolute best decision was absolutely crippling us. I decided that our process needed to be to eliminate the bad decisions, and then make a decision!

Keep Your Foot Soldiers As Strident Believers

As a company blossoms into a sizeable organization, it actually becomes more essential than ever before that the company's foot soldiers are still strident believers in the firm's visionary creed. For some reason, though, there seems to be a pervasive attitude inside many technology-focused businesses that once the business is assured of survival and success its foot soldiers don't matter as much. The company will still offer them nice benefits and even throw a Christmas party once a year, but for the most part the company doesn't believe its foot soldiers, having served their purpose, are worth paying much attention to anymore.

Clearly, nothing could be further from the truth! In case any of us may have forgotten, the foot soldiers in any digital business are typically the workers who have the closest day-to-day relationships with customers. A company's CEO may be smiling in his executive suite, but it will be the demoralized and even angry faces of his foot soldiers that the customers see. If your tech support team, customer service representatives, and salespeople stop believing in your company's greater vision to change the entire world, it is likely that your company's own little world is destined to come to an abrupt standstill.

Think about what would happen tomorrow if Amazon's thousands of warehouse workers abruptly decided that Jeff Bezos was clueless about the company's future and had no plan for the company reaching profitability. For all intents and purposes Amazon would be shut down. And it's not just the risk of being crippled operationally that makes it so important that your foot soldiers remain strong believers. Companies that don't follow this step in the hyper-growth process are susceptible to high levels of employee turnover and visible fumbling of the ball by the organization, not to mention significantly higher training and recruitment costs.

Unfortunately, this continues to be an area where many young tech businesses struggle. Instead of investing the time and resources needed to keep their companies' foot soldiers well informed, many now defunct dot-com companies devoted their time to churning out partnership announcements and launching flashy ad campaigns. While this strategy kept employees satisfied during the gravy days of the tech sector, it exploded in their faces during the industry's subsequent shakeout.

So don't think for a second that foot soldiers can't sense inherent strength or weakness in your company's leadership. They know. They won't be your pawns on a chessboard. Keep their faith or risk having your troops desert you during heavy combat, as Internet.com's Alan Meckler reminds us.

ALAN MECKLER

Chief Executive Officer and Founder of INTMedia Corp.

Q **Ragas:** Some of the biggest and most successful digital companies of all time—ranging from Microsoft to Yahoo—practically had their own distinct "religion" in a sense. Everyone believed deeply in the mission and task at hand. Do you have any insights into how a company can inject this same sense of passion and trust into its own organization?

A **Meckler:** Particularly in the Internet sector, winning the respect and trust of all the foot soldiers and officers in your organization is crucial. They must believe you really do have a quality product or service. Up until maybe a year ago, it was very easy for employees to jump from one company to another for stock options. A lot of that stock option euphoria has now been taken away. The fact is that, as it gets tighter and more difficult in the marketplace, it's even more important that a company's employees believe the senior people know what they're doing. I think this is one of the big problems in the Internet sector. When things go bad, workers quickly begin to doubt their company's future and leave, because they don't have any faith in the management team's ability to build a real business!

Q **Ragas:** Well, lack of faith in an organization's management has definitely led to the downfall of a number of digital companies when they were forced to endure a tough stretch. Instead of sticking it out, a lot of the foot soldiers at dot-coms with weak business models just decided to surrender!

A **Meckler:** Yes. Leadership in the Internet space is more important than it has ever been in any industry to date. It's the same thing in the military in a combat situation. You're more likely to put your life on the line to save somebody if you think your lieutenant is good at heart and that he wouldn't send you out to do something that was just absolutely insane. I'm a strong believer that what's been learned in the military is particularly important in the tech sector, because I consider Internet growth and leadership to be a lot like com-

> *"I'm absolutely convinced that the closest thing to combat in business that we've ever seen is the Internet arena."*

bat. I'm absolutely convinced that the closest thing to combat in business that we've ever seen is the Internet arena. That's why we have no secretaries in our company and everybody has a direct-dial phone number. Having the entire company adopt this combat leadership approach is really the key. Unfortunately, I think many Internet companies don't have this mentality at all!

Don't Be Afraid to Expand and Contract

Even an organization that has kept its foot soldiers as strident believers and accepted the fact that it cannot make the absolute best management decisions has still not successfully climbed all the way to the top of the mountain. Like an expert mountain climber, a rapidly growing company needs different tools and resources at different stages of the climb, and the choice of these all depends on the type of mountain that is being scaled. Pack too heavy and the climber could become overburdened and die; pack too light and the climber could leave out a lifesaving rope. In this same way, the most successful digital companies are constantly assessing and reassessing their operational and human-capital needs.

Some level of expanding and contracting is a fact of life in any rapidly growing technology-focused business. While layoffs are never a pleasant subject, when done properly job reductions are a healthy way to help balance out the needs and goals of an organization. Bloated companies help no one. They aren't good for streamlined decision making, and they certainly aren't good for serving customers, since they typically only offer layer after layer of bureaucracy. Unfortunately, piles of venture capital have their way of making even the hungriest startups become fat and lazy virtually overnight. A job that originally took one person eight hours to do becomes expanded into a team project now magically requiring three people. Don't let this kind of hyper-growth laziness creep into your own organization!

Conduct performance reviews of your organization at least once a quarter. Trim the fat. Unless you're still operating out of your garage or basement, fat exists. Companies are much like an organism with constantly evolving needs. This means that the head-count formula that worked at one point in the company's life cycle isn't likely to work the same way the next time. The human-capital component of your organization is constantly changing. Maybe you don't need as many software engineers or developers as you once did, but then again maybe you need more.

You get the idea. Analyze your human-capital infrastructure. Regularly fine-tune it. Expand it. Contract it. Don't be afraid to make the tough decisions. As much as any successful digital company may feel like a family, remember it is still a business. As hard as it is for us to admit, even some family members overextend their welcome once in a while. Demand performance and reward performance, but cut the organizational freeloaders. At the end of the day, your stakeholders expect and deserve nothing less than the best, as PurchasePro's Junior Johnson helps crystallize.

CHARLES JOHNSON JR.

Founder, Chairman, and
Chief Executive Officer of PurchasePro.com

Q **Ragas:** We have seen a significant amount of layoffs and scaling back of operations across the tech landscape in the past year as companies try to streamline their operations. What lessons do you have for companies that are still grappling with the issue of further expanding or contracting their business?

A **Johnson:** What happened to us was, we originally hired very, very fast. When this happens, it means that your company will likely expand and then contract. Each quarter you need to look at each area that you expanded and then decide to either expand it further or contract it. We're probably the only dot-com company in history to double its revenue and lower its head count. This is where it gets down to really running a business. In my previous businesses, I had combined among all of my companies close to twelve hundred employees. I learned you really have to have the right people at the right place at the right time for the right reason to be successful. And this mix changes every day. What happens with most companies is that they expand very fast and hire people to meet the need at hand and then eventually this need goes down, and twice as many people end up doing the same amount of work.

Q **Ragas:** Right. As a business continues to evolve, its human-capital needs are constantly evolving and changing as well. Companies must get over the mental hurdle that somehow laying off employees is always a bad thing. While this part of the process never feels good, it's part of business. Organizations must constantly review the current human-capital needs in each facet of their workforce and adjust accordingly.

A **Johnson:** Companies really should do regular employee reviews based on performance as well as company need. Performance is a big issue, because companies hire very rapidly and just can't hire 100 percent perfectly. Even knowing this, though, most people won't make the tough decision to purge. We did. We've lowered head count before. In our case, this was due to lack of employee performance and areas where we didn't need as many people anymore. We run the business to make money. Layoffs are always a tough decision

"You really have to have the right people at the right place at the right time for the right reason to be successful."

that everybody hates to make, but it's the real world. I always ask my people, "If this was 100 percent your money, what would you do?" When they figure out their money is also at stake, it makes a big difference!

MASTERING THE MEDIA MACHINE

EVEN THE FAMOUS SHOWMAN AND ILLUSTRIOUS ENTREPRENEUR P.T. Barnum would likely find it difficult to break through all of the clutter in today's crowded technology marketplace. After being bombarded for years by hare-brained gimmicks and outlandish publicity stunts, people today would not feel the same awe as the sight of Barnum's bearded lady or the Siamese twins created over 150 years ago. Today's public and media have grown hardened to the smoke and mirrors of the publicity gimmicks that are all too common in the tech marketplace.

Barnum may or may not have uttered the famous line, "There's a sucker born every minute." If he were alive today, he might say instead, "There's a dishonest company tarred and feathered every second." The only sucker in today's digital world is the company that believes that with the right

...e an inferior product or service
amount of spin it words. The slimy spinmeister and
seem enticing. Melong to an endangered species des-
the corporate c in the dodo bird in extinction.
tined eventual companies will never be able to reform
Sad to sa ways as hard as they may try, because their
their spinme has been built upon one mountain of spin after
entire comp onest technology-focused companies, however,
another. F ear se of steps that they can follow to successfully
there is a immdiate impact with the press and maintain this
make mon ntum or the long haul. I will share with you in this chap-
te che keys to mastering the media machine and the attention
of the general public without any smoke and mirrors or dash of
snake oil, but with integrity, honor, and most important, trust.

As Launch.com's Dave Goldberg will remind us, no really
good relationship is built overnight. Winning trust with key
industry writers, analysts, and commentators takes a serious
investment of time and effort and is the first step in the publicity process. Ways that companies can plug into existing mega
media waves in the marketplace and ride them for all they're
worth will be discussed next, with help from McAfee ASaP
chief Zach Nelson. As you will see, riding these waves is much
easier if your company has a compelling and unique story to tell
to the public. Naveen Jain of InfoSpace will expound on this
power of being unique and different in the eyes of the media.

After building a unique story to tell to the media and industry analysts, the successful digital company has just begun its
job. With Powered Computing founder Michael Rosenfelt we
will explore the importance of deciding when to shoot your
buzz bullets and when to keep your hand off the P.R. trigger.
After all, hardly any company is given an unlimited number of
shots at making a lasting impression with key industry influencers and the public. Finally, I will review, with supporting
thoughts from Go2Net founder Russ Horowitz, a final step

companies can take to make sure they are using real substance to back up the market perception that they have created.

Build Relationships with Key Industry Writers, Commentators, and Analysts

The first step in successfully making an impact in the media is to understand that the best things in life often come to those who wait. Receiving a boatload of press attention is not a magical process that happens overnight. A company does not simply step into a phone booth and come out a minute later dressed as a magical super business that every journalist in the country is itching to write about. Realize from the get-go that garnering significant media attention is a relationship game like anything else in business, and it takes time and effort to build these meaningful relationships.

When I say meaningful relationships, I'm not simply talking about mailing press kits to influential analysts and writers or incessantly ringing their phones to say how wonderful your company is! In fact, that's a great way never to receive serious press attention. Taking key industry commentators out to lunch or dinner isn't likely to do the trick, either. Remember, these are people who are used to being wined and dined by executives who want something. Most of them have forgotten more story pitches than you'll think of in your lifetime!

Instead, focus your efforts on letting analysts and writers know that your executives and founders are always available to comment on broad trends and popular issues in your industry. Transform your company into a readily available resource for commenting on industry events. While this isn't a glamorous approach and it won't seem to pay off with immediate dividends, it is the best way to build confidence and trust in selected members of the press. Make them your friends, and they are ten times more likely to consider writing about your company or a new product launch when you have a serious announcement to make.

There are a couple of ways to help speed up your relationship with the media. Top-tier venture capital firms are phenomenal gatekeepers to the press, so that an investment in your company by one of these firms generally has the result of significantly greasing the press machine's wheels. In addition, bringing aboard a public relations whiz very early on in your company's formation can be beneficial as well. Your whiz should have an established track record in your industry and a legitimate list of press contacts. For the most part, though, as Launch's Dave Goldberg attests, the key to starting out on a good footing with the media is to spend the necessary time and effort to cultivate lasting relationships.

DAVID GOLDBERG

Founder, Chief Executive Officer,
and Chairman of Launch Media

Q **Ragas:** As a writer, I am regularly bombarded with press releases from lots of different tech companies, many of whom have never picked up the phone to call me or sent me a personalized e-mail. Do you have any insights into building relationships with the media to help companies break through the clutter?

A **Goldberg:** Well, this has been a very interesting challenge for our company because we're not located in Silicon Valley. We're based in Los Angeles, which is not exactly the center of the technology universe. What's worked for us is to consistently show results to the media. This helps prove that we're really building a good business. I also think it's important for companies to spend time talking to the media and industry people that they think are really smart. I've spent a lot of time helping people understand our business, even though my efforts haven't necessarily translated into a particular story about us on that day. Spending time is still important because, eventually, when you do have something you want to talk to them about, they will trust you because you've been building a relationship all along. A lot of times I'm never mentioned in a story, but I spend the time to help the writer get a perspective on what's happening in our business. It's an investment of time on my part, and it's worth it, because when I do go to them with something, I know what they're interested in. In other words, I don't go and pitch them on just any random press release. I go to them and say, "We've got this really important announcement about something that I think

> *"Don't waste media people's time! Companies should spend a lot of time learning what particular journalists want to write about."*

you're going to be interested in." Don't waste media people's time! Companies should spend a lot of time learning what particular journalists want to write about.

Plug Your Company into the Mega-Media Wave

There is a lot to be said for not trying to swim against the tide and to go with the flow whenever possible. Garnering favorable media attention is no different. Assuming that you have invested the time and effort to build solid press relationships, it is now time to look around your company's marketplace. What are the broader mainstream trends, issues, and events taking place in your market that broadcasters and writers are covering? Who and what are currently showing up on the covers of the trade magazines in your industry? What industry-wide issues are people buzzing about at cocktail parties?

After you answer these questions, you can begin to position your company as the solution or educator to a problem, issue, or phenomenon that is taking place in your firm's broader market. In other words, instead of creating your own wave from scratch, focus your efforts on finding ways to plug your company into an existing mega-media wave and then ride it for all its worth. In the late nineties, for example, Linux software company Red Hat, by positioning itself as the anti-Microsoft, was masterful at exploiting the frenetic media coverage surrounding Microsoft and its alleged monopoly behavior into reams of positive press for itself.

The success of the *Blair Witch Project* Web site in creating incredible buzz for that movie is another example of plugging into an existing mega-media wave. While the *Blair Witch* incident happened largely by accident, it coincided with the media's hunger in 1999 for a tangible example for average people to understand the broad impact the Internet was having on society. Amazingly, the movie ended up being the cover stories of both *Time* and *Newsweek* both in the same week!

Unfortunately, most technology-focused companies still seem hell-bent on trying to blaze company-specific public relations trails, even when the exploitable broader trends are right under their noses. So sit down with your marketing department and a stack of the latest industry publications and some mainstream weekly news magazines and plot out on paper the emerging trends or issues journalists seem to be interested in. Chances are that somewhere in this mass of news and opinion will be a trend your company can ride to your own media attention, as McAfee ASaP's Zach Nelson cleverly notes.

ZACH NELSON

Chief Executive Officer and President of McAfee ASaP; former Vice President of Worldwide Marketing, Oracle

Q **Ragas:** It's no big secret that getting media attention in today's crowded digital marketplace is becoming increasingly difficult. Every company is yelling and screaming for attention. What advice do you have for breaking through all this clutter?

A **Nelson:** It's tough to break through the enormous amount of clutter out there. One of the great things we did when we first launched MyCIO.com [now called McAfee ASaP] is that we draped our entire eleven-story building on Highway 101 with the MyCIO.com logo. It was the world's largest billboard. The city of San Jose wasn't very happy with us for doing it, but they let us keep it up for a month. Everyone that I called after we ran that giant billboard I received a return call back from. You do have to think out of the box while thinking on message at the same time,

> *"Companies should think about how they can plug into trends and ride those trends, and that will gain favorable reviews of their product or service in the press."*

though. You really can't do it with advertising alone because it's too expensive. So it has to be something that is not only memorable, but sustaining. Another thing that we have as an advantage in our marketplace—the network security sector—is that there are always buzz issues that come up, like a new virus or denial of service attack. We're fortunate enough to have solutions we can post on our Web site to cure those problems instantly. Companies should think about how they can plug into trends and ride those trends, and that will gain favorable reviews of their product or service in the press. Sometimes you have to look at what the bigger wave is and see how or if your company can plug into it or even find a way to take that wave down. Don't forget that reporters always have to report both sides of the picture. I always look for leverage issues, like our security solutions, for example, where we not only tell the media what we're doing but also offer a solution to the problem that they're writing about.

Does Your Company Have a Compelling Story to Tell?

Once you have identified existing mega-media trends already taking place or beginning to bubble up in your marketplace, it is important to start thinking like a reporter. In other words, if you were writing an article or column, what would be the really compelling story surrounding your company that your industry or even the general public really care about? Take your time and be creative. Don't even think about using the tired angle that your company simply has "the best product or service in the world." While this might be the case, this approach is a surefire way to step right into the noise of the marketplace and get yourself completely ignored by the press.

Keep in mind that reporters hear virtually non-stop each day from spinmeisters babbling on about how revolutionary their products or services are. That's why veteran journalists are generally the biggest group of doubting Thomases in the world. I can't blame them. Unless they can see and feel your revolutionary new product or service with their own eyes and hands, they are going to disregard your claims that "we're the best" or "we're the first." Instead, your company must approach this situation from the angle of how you are unique and different.

Even if your CEO doesn't ride a Harley Davidson motorcycle or skydive out of planes on the weekend, chances are there is something distinctly unique and different about your business. If there isn't, then your company probably shouldn't have been started in the first place, and I doubt this is the case. You just need to dig deep. Really deep. Stimulate discussion in your company, and you will come up with a list of unique and compelling story angles about your business.

Remember, choose a story angle that is so compelling that a reporter can't afford to not write about your business.

If you've got a story that is different and unique, you are going to help sell newspapers and boost television ratings, and from that time forward you will have a friend in the media. As InfoSpace's Naveen Jain craftily reminds us, the media need compelling stories just as much as digital companies need the media!

NAVEEN JAIN

Founder and Chairman of InfoSpace, Inc.;
former Group Manager of Microsoft

Q **Ragas:** Some technology-focused companies are great at garnering media attention, but most are lousy at differentiating themselves from the rest of the pack. What are some of the keys to getting industry analysts and market pundits to take notice of a company and its product or service?

A **Jain:** We have never had an outside public relations person or an outside public relations company work for us here at InfoSpace. It is just too important a job to give to someone else. What I've learned is that the media needs you just as much as you need the media. They are always looking for a new compelling story. You as a company have to not only have a new compelling story, but you also have to look at the story from their perspective. Always ask yourself, Why should a reporter be interested in what my company is doing? I've found that being a little different, while also being yourself, is what really gets great media attention. You need to give a reporter a reason to write about you. Let me give you an example. When a reporter asked me very simply, "So why did you decide to leave Microsoft?" I could have come up with a number of different answers, but my simple one-liner was, "I got tired of making billions for Bill!" At the beginning of that interview, all the reporter was trying to do was to write a story

"I've found that being a little different, while also being yourself, is what really gets great media attention."

about Microsoft. Instead, the story ended up being about InfoSpace, because I gave the reporter a compelling new angle to write about. What I'm saying is that many, many times people have called me up just to get a quote for some other company's story, and it turns out they write the entire story on InfoSpace! To be successful you just need to give the media a new, compelling story each time.

Make Your Buzz Bullets Count

After developing a compelling story for the media and identifying mega-media waves, it is important not to turn into the boy who cried wolf! Cherish the press and industry analyst relationships that you have worked so hard to cultivate and build. Be careful not to blanket them with every run-of-the-mill press release your marketing department or outside public relations firm churns out. Be selective about how and when you leverage your contacts and industry influencers. Otherwise, no one will pay attention to your company when you have something important to say.

Take good care of the unique and compelling story pitches your company has crafted. Protect your buzz bullets and choose very carefully when to fire a round or two and, equally important, when to holster your weapon. Chances are, your company will not have an unlimited supply of ammunition! Try to shoot at too many media targets at once, and you'll end up having the whole media crowd think you're out of control, unfocused, and not worth their time. In addition, influential industry commentators, writers, and analysts love to feel and be treated like special people, so learn to treat them like royalty or pay the price.

While it might not always seem fair, realize from the start that this select class of media and industry analysts expects to regularly receive the inside scoop and nothing less. You can play by their rules or go home. It's always going to be a lot harder to convince them they are still the big cheese when your public relations people are promiscuously firing buzz bullets all over the place. Stop. Don't let this happen. Ever. Be patient and wait for the right moment to take your best shots. Otherwise, the net result will be that your company is good at making a loud noise, but after a while everyone stops listening, as Powered founder Michael Rosenfelt helps hammer home.

MICHAEL ROSENFELT

Founder of Powered, Inc.;
Venture Partner, Impact Venture Partners

Q **Ragas:** Building buzz is a unique mix of art and science. Those companies that are really good at it often find it opens doors to a variety of business opportunities. Keeping this in mind, what are your thoughts on the best ways to build and sustain buzz around a company's new product or service?

A **Rosenfelt:** Buzz properly applied and properly deployed is a very powerful strategic weapon. Buzz for buzz's sake is a wasted cycle, though, and becomes a waste of energy and time. Invariably, it will backfire. Let me give you a real-world example about Powered, Inc. Shortly after we founded the company, we were negotiating with several venture capital firms to lead our first round of financing. In the midst of these term sheet negotiations, a cover story on our company appeared in the local paper, the *Austin American Statesman,* which is very influential in the Southwest for technology coverage. That cover story led to an ensuing feeding frenzy behind the ultimate valuation of our financing. There is this perception, rightly or wrongly, that media coverage and attention create credibility and legitimacy. But you want to be smart about how and when you use your bullets.

Q **Ragas:** Media and analyst coverage definitely does initially create an aura of credibility around a new company or a new product or service. At the end of the day, though, the company still has to deliver on its promises and use buzz carefully, or it can find that it has accidentally knocked over a huge hornet's nest!

A **Rosenfelt:** Yes. Most important, you have to understand what's the really compelling story behind your company. Ask yourself, is it the management, the market, the company's investors, or a trend in the marketplace that you should capitalize upon? Companies need to have the ability to boil their compelling story down into a couple of key bullets. A good story will invariably revolve around conflict and change, because that's what makes for interesting news. Getting good media coverage is also about building relationships, but relationships are probably less important than a really, really good story. Great public relations are crucial. In fact, with every company I've ever founded or consulted, I always want someone there with public relations experience from day one. I want them there thinking about how this story is going to play with analysts and the press.

"You have to understand what's the really compelling story behind your company."

Back Up Perception with Substance

Earlier in this chapter I pointed out that we are in an environment today in which dishonest companies are quickly found out and then tarred and feathered. The days of forgive and forget are over. The media and the public have simply been burned far too many times to swallow a company's magic elixir without proof of its effectiveness. I don't care if your company's spinmeisters are as smooth as silk or as cunning as a cat. Unless there is real underlying substance to your P.R. message, you will eventually be exposed. Every spin machine must face the music today. Are you prepared? I hope so.

The last few years marked a unique era in the history of the tech sector. During this crazy period, companies were able to use favorable media attention to raise venture capital, close high-profile alliances, and in some extreme cases, ride the buzz all the way to an IPO. While I've learned never to say "never," those gravy days are far behind us, at least for the foreseeable future. Every dream eventually comes to an end. Perception can create windows of opportunity, but marketplace perception must sooner or later be backed up with real substance. Otherwise, the public and the press will react with more fury and rage against your organization, and you will pay a heavy price.

Take troubled dot-com company TheGlobe.com, for example. When this fledgling firm went public in November of 1998, it enjoyed one of the most impressive opening day IPO performances of all time. The company received phenomenal media attention as part of this news. Its young founders, Stephan Paternot and Todd Krizelman, appeared on numerous magazine covers and television news shows. However, over the next two years, as the company struggled to make financial projections and deliver on promises, the media quickly turned and used TheGlobe.com as the poster child for the "dot-com bubble."

While TheGlobe.com is an extreme example, numerous tech companies have eventually been pummeled into a coma or even put to death by the media for using frothy publicity to inflate expectations. That's why I can't stress enough the importance of your business being extremely careful about what it does and doesn't say to the media or the public.

People remember more quickly the promises someone has broken than the ones they may have kept. Think before your company speaks!

Never forget that credibility is king and the foundation of your company's castle. Don't allow your organization to say things it will regret later and become the next rising star to be blinded by the media spotlight. Take precautions. Under-promise and over-deliver. Ignore the temptation to say what the media wants to hear, as Go2Net founder Russ Horowitz so succinctly stresses.

RUSSELL HOROWITZ

Founder and Former Chairman of Go2Net, Inc.

Q **Ragas:** I don't think anyone would disagree that a number of companies in the tech sector in the past few years have been masters at leveraging positive media attention into the signing of high-profile alliances and partnerships. With this in mind, what lesson do you have on utilizing public relations as an offensive weapon in the marketplace?

A **Horowitz:** I characterize everything in business by windows of opportunity. These windows come in all different forms, and the impact of successful public relations and investor relations in this industry should not be underestimated. For this reason, companies have to be careful to distinguish between communicating a message that has substance behind it and just spreading hype. Companies need to remember that the message can always change, but integrity and credibility don't. Once you lose your credibility, you're done! So it's one thing to communicate a message that creates a perception that in turn leads to an opportunity, but unless there's some credibility to it, you will be held accountable. To the extent that your credibility suffers as a result of this behavior, your ability to compete going forward is compromised.

Q **Ragas:** Right. At times, perception eventually does turn into reality, but it can just as easily blow up in your face, unless there is real substance behind all the glowing press releases your company has been cranking out. In other words, perpetrators will be found and shot!

A **Horowitz:** We've had plenty of opportunities throughout the history of our company to say what people wanted to hear, but we knew this didn't have any real substance, so we shied away from it. I'm not trying to hold us up on a pedestal, but I think we've done a good job of avoiding some of the immediate gratification that was available to us by saying what the media or Wall Street wanted to hear. Companies must realize that the fundamental task in public relations is to establish and then enhance their credibility. They should never do anything to compromise that!

"Companies must realize that the fundamental task in public relations is to establish and then enhance their credibility."

CHAPTER 11

NAVIGATING NEGOTIATIONS AND PARTNERSHIPS

IF BUSINESS IS LIKE WAR, THEN ONE NEEDS TO LOOK NO FURTHER than the recent battle of capitalism versus communism to witness the incredible power that effective alliances and partnerships can have in toppling the competition. For roughly forty-five years, the Cold War dominated world affairs and kept the two most powerful nations in the world on near constant red alert. The challenge of trying to keep a cash-strapped startup or ailing corporation afloat seems almost laughable in comparison. From 1946 to 1989, the world very much teetered on the brink of Armageddon. Weapons of mass destruction were stockpiled. Desperate plans to survive nuclear attacks were crafted. Both sides constantly threatened to press "the red button." What caused the Soviet Union's ultimate undoing were unbreakable alliances between the United States and Western Europe, as

well as daring Eastern European political activists. Words—
not weapons—eventually won the day.

Achieving success in the Next Economy is really no different. In fact, with the tech marketplace now more crowded
and frenetic than ever before, long-lasting partnerships and
alliances have become crucial for achieving clear market dominance. Markets can rarely be captured and protected by solo
companies anymore. Look at the informal alliance that chip
titan Intel and software giant Microsoft have enjoyed. While
the famed Wintel duopoly now shows some signs of cracking,
this strategic alliance has allowed both firms to maintain a
near stranglehold grip over the entire PC industry for years.

For every Wintel-like partnership that has been successfully crafted, there are probably at least a thousand or more
just as promising alliances that have amounted to little more
than marketing hype. These were deals with lots of sizzle but
no steak. We've all seen these types of hare-brained deals or
experienced them firsthand. Yet the deal-making game doesn't
have to turn to failure, and in this chapter I will provide you
with a proven game plan for navigating the tricky world of
negotiations and partnerships. As you will see, alliances can
indeed still be formed in Internet time and actually last. To
begin this alliance-building process, we will first explore—
with accompanying thoughts from Jeff Smith of Tumbleweed
and Martin Tobias of Loudeye—the importance of fomenting
demand in the marketplace for your company's product or
service. Next, Aptimus founder Tim Choate will reinforce the
importance of keeping a company's reputation squeaky clean
when the time comes to hit the negotiating table. Of course,
no formal deal should be announced until it is first tested in
the field, as Art Technology CEO Jeet Singh will point out.

Finally, I will wrap up the chapter with 24/7 Media's
Dave Moore explaining the importance of finding the proper
chemistry between your organization and a potential

partner. After all, deals based solely on numbers look great, but if you can't get along with the people behind the numbers, the partnership or alliance will more than likely hurt both sides.

Value Chain First, Partnerships Later

The first step in creating successful alliances and partnerships in any business is to understand where your company sits in the industry's value chain. Until you can clearly identify what piece or section of the value chain your business dominates (or has at least a secure footing in) any major deals are a waste of time. America Online wasn't able to start doing really significant deals with traditional media companies until it became clear that AOL was king or at least prince of the online services world. Until AOL had carved out this position in the consumer Internet value chain, the media companies had little incentive to do serious business with AOL.

Most alliances for early stage companies typically don't end up amounting to very much, because the fledgling firm has very little value to offer a larger prospective partner. In fact, this prospective partner may just as likely want to enter the business that you're already in on its own—without you. That's why it's so important to realize that an immature market is a lot like a game of musical chairs. Everyone is moving around looking for the best seat in the marketplace. This is why deals between two immature companies are about as useful as two ants joining forces to tote a loaf of bread!

It makes much more sense for fledgling companies to hold off on trying to make a deal and instead focus full force on creating a clearly unassailable and insurmountable part of the value chain first. Secure this position, and your organization will have a centerpiece of power to offer to potential business partners. Deals built solely on pixie dust and promises and no transfer of value for both parties might as well be thrown into the trash heap before they are even signed. As Loudeye founder Martin Tobias reminds us, a Machiavellian approach to deal making today is flawed: Both parties must see tangible incentives for making a deal work.

MARTIN TOBIAS
Founder and Chairman of Loudeye Technologies

Q **Ragas:** The tech sector is littered with failed partnerships and glitzy press releases announcing alliances that don't pan out. At the same time, though, the age of companies doing everything on their own is over. So what lessons have you learned about structuring successful alliances as a young company?

A **Tobias:** Partnerships are especially difficult in an early market where not everyone is sure who sits where in the value chain and what part of the value chain is going to emerge as the most important. When you're in that kind of a market, you see everyone jockeying for the best position. Everyone wants to play musical chairs and not sit still in one place. While you are trying to partner with someone, that same company may also be looking at actually getting into your business, if your business seems to be better than their business. In early markets, I've found that partnerships really don't work well at all. In mature markets, deals tend to work better, but only after you have built a clearly unassailable or valuable part of the value chain that is hard for someone else to replicate. That's why in digital media services, Loudeye is far and away the largest. When you're the largest, people have to deal with you! So the first thing a company must do if they want to have strong partners is to create a strong value proposition in their core product. If you haven't created that value and demand in the marketplace yet, then you're not going to be valuable to anyone as a partner.

Q **Ragas:** Young companies must firmly establish their product or service as the hands-down leader in one segment or piece of the value chain. Only then will other players in the value chain feel compelled to strike even-handed and fair deals with you.

A **Tobias:** Yes. The first thing companies need to realize is that almost every business is part of a larger value chain. There are almost always related companies in a market who do complementary things for your customers. In the streaming media sector where our company is, there is definitely a clear value chain. We have a couple of key alliances. We are doing audio and video-encoding work, which when completed, goes to a hosted Web network like Akamai or Digital Island. We definitely have to have partnership relationships with Akamai and Digital Island, because they are an essential part of a complete solution for our customers who have to buy both hosting and encoding services. Companies must first discover who in their market the other key companies in the value chain really are and only then try and form relationships with them. These relationships will only work if they are win-win. You must have incentives for both companies to make money off the same customers if you really want a partnership or alliance to succeed!

"Deals tend to work . . . only after you have built a clearly unassailable or valuable part of the value chain."

Demand in the Marketplace Makes for Lasting Partnerships

Even after reading this last piece of advice, I'm sure there are some executives out there rushing to craft any deal they can do. Sadly, signing deals is all that many upstart companies know how to do—or at least think they know how to do. The trouble is, hype and flash in the deal-making arena can only last for so long. While this behavior might be good enough to snare a few beta customers and some bubbly press mentions, it is bound to eventually fizzle out like a stale glass of champagne. This is why your company must hold a real value proposition to the market, or the other participants in your value chain will eventually eat you alive.

This is exactly what happened to many early-stage, business-to-business Internet companies that were developing industry-specific, online exchanges and marketplaces. These B-to-B startups all hastily signed up traditional bricks-and-mortar companies to become participants in their online exchanges. When it became time for these bricks-and-mortar companies to start conducting some of their transactions online, many of them decided it made more sense to build their own exchanges. In other words, many of these early B-to-B marketplace companies ended up getting knocked out of the value chain because they couldn't offer visible value in the marketplace when they crafted partnerships.

This example shows that getting partnerships to stick is extremely difficult unless you can offer lasting value to your prospective partner. Until the customers of your potential partners come up to them and tell them how much they enjoy or need your product or service, your company is not ready for the partnership big leagues. However, if you do not see this "need" expressed yet from potential partners, it is not necessarily a bad thing. It's much better to realize where you stand than to operate in a state of denial.

Like it or not, a company must have at least one clearly defined core competency that other organizations desire to tap into before it can ever hope to craft lasting deals. This may sound harsh, but it's simple reality. Fact and fiction eventually end up getting separated in almost every situation. While "Barney deals" may be great for creating lots of initial smiles and hearty laughs, these hot-air-filled partnership dances don't end up creating long-lasting companies, as Tumbleweed's Jeff Smith reminds us.

JEFFREY SMITH

Founder, Chief Executive Officer,
and President of Tumbleweed Communications

Q **Ragas:** Many private and some public companies today seem fixated on signing as many partnerships and alliances as possible, because they believe that this behavior somehow enhances their visibility and credibility. As you know, though, the majority of deals in the digital universe fail. What lessons do you have on partnerships?

A **Smith:** I think there are two factors that come into play here. A partnership has to benefit both sides or it just won't work. This sounds obvious, but it is so true. If you are a smaller company, there are only a few things you're doing that are of real benefit to a larger company. As a small company, you might think, "Great. We can approach Oracle and put together a partnership!" But why does Oracle care? How is that partnership you're trying to cut going to benefit Oracle? Big companies already have plenty of fish to fry. In the case of Oracle, they have one of the largest sales organizations in the world. If they really needed the technology your company could provide in a partnership, why wouldn't they just go off and build it themselves? Most partnerships for most early stage companies are what I call "Barney deals." When I say Barney, I'm referring to the purple dragon from the popular children's television show that kind of bounces around but doesn't really do anything. Barney just smiles and sings happy songs!

Q **Ragas:** Right. Doing a deal for a deal's sake with a larger corporation is a waste of time if your business has yet to firmly establish its product or service as a value proposition already readily accepted and demanded by the marketplace. There must be a real incentive already apparent for the larger partner to want to follow through.

A **Smith:** Yes. Real deals have to benefit both sides. Look at Oracle again. Why is Oracle going to care about a partnership? They're going to care about something if their customers tell them they need it. When are their customers going to tell them they need it? The customer is going to tell them they need it when they are already educated about this product or service and are buying it from somebody else. What makes partnerships particularly difficult is that usually there isn't demand from the customer side for early-stage products. This demand must be developed in the field first, either through aggressive selling and aggressive marketing or some combination of the two. It may sound cynical, but partnerships really don't matter until a company is large enough and strong enough to create a win-win scenario for both sides. That takes time.

> *"Most partnerships for most early stage companies are what I call 'Barney deals.'...Real deals have to benefit both sides."*

Reputation Means Everything

After firmly establishing demand in the marketplace for your company's product or service, it is important to try to establish true win-win relationships. The easiest way to begin this process is to enter any potential negotiation with an already upstanding reputation among your organization's stakeholders. Credible companies emit trust and integrity. Become this type of organization. This is not something that I can magically do for you, but if you already have been trustworthy and credible with existing suppliers, customers, investors, and the media, you should already have the foundation of a solid reputation in place.

Think for a second why having an upstanding reputation is so crucial at the bargaining table. Alliances are largely agreements in which both sides make and then keep promises. As a young company, there is little else for an established potential partner to use in sizing up the integrity of your business than an industry-wide assessment of your firm's reputation in the marketplace. If your firm's reputation is full of broken promises, there is no reason a sensible partner would want to sit down with you. It would be a waste of their time.

Data analysis software company MicroStrategy has experienced firsthand the fallout surrounding the results of broken promises and a tarnished reputation. By early 2000, MicroStrategy was one of the hottest software companies in the world with a valuation of $26 billion dollars and a stock price that had risen 2,600 percent from its IPO price. Soon thereafter, though, incredibly damaging reports were released admitting that the company had been falsely inflating its revenue totals for three years. In sum, MicroStrategy executives ended up having to pay $10 million in fines and penalties to the Securities and Exchange Commission.

As one can imagine, MicroStrategy's reputation, which it had worked so hard to cultivate for almost a decade among customers, partners, investors, and employees, was annihilated virtually overnight. While MicroStrategy still exists today and is recovering from this costly setback, the fact remains that it is extremely difficult to ever fully repair a tarnished reputation. Keep this in mind, and do whatever it takes to make sure your own organization guards its reputation with its life. Intellectual property is nice, but a company's reputation is its most precious asset, according to Aptimus founder Tim Choate, and I certainly won't disagree with him on that.

TIM CHOATE

Founder and Chief Executive Officer of Aptimus;
former Vice President of Micro Warehouse

Q **Ragas:** Tech companies are notorious for signing deals that only a month or two later end up being meaningless and a waste of time. Do you have any ground rules to share with entrepreneurs and executives about forming long-lasting and enduring alliances?

A **Choate:** I'm a firm believer in forming true win-win and positive relationships. For example, most of the companies that we do partnerships with here at Aptimus are very friendly with us, and we've worked with them over the years. If you're very friendly, when you find problems—because you invariably will—you can work together to get through them, as opposed to having an antagonistic relationship where you work together at not getting problems solved. One of the things I've noticed is that the technology and Internet business is a fairly small community. Everyone more or less knows everyone else. In the Internet industry there is a much smaller separation between companies. The news of a bad relationship between two companies spreads very quickly to everyone else in the tech industry. Frequently, a company hears about bad previous relationships with a potential partner that they are considering working with and then they back away from that potential deal. The deal collapses before it even had a chance to start!

Q **Ragas:** Right. The Internet is such a hyper-growth environment that companies don't waste their time exploring potential partnerships with a firm that they may have heard bad things about previously. There just isn't the time in this business for organizations to fool around with stepping on potential land mines.

A **Choate:** To me, one of the absolute keys in this business is to have good relationships with partners that start with an honest

"The news of a bad relationship between two companies spreads very quickly to everyone else in the tech industry."

win-win foundation. I have a very, very high hit-rate on getting a deal done if I set out to do it. Part of that is because I enter any deal with a high degree of open-mindedness. I sit in the meeting and say. "Okay. What is this guy really looking for? What am I really looking for? How can we bring those two things together?" As the meeting progresses, companies should always try and figure out what the real hot-button issues are and how the two companies' strategies can come together in a way that works well for everyone.

Never Try to Force Feed a Partnership

After focusing on protecting your company's reputation, the next step in the partnership building process is to focus on doing deals that make sense not just in the boardroom—but out in the field as well. Just because an alliance looks wonderful to a dozen people in a stuffy conference room doesn't mean it will appear nearly as splendid to an overworked software engineer sitting in a cubicle farm or a salesperson located in a satellite office halfway around the world. Unfortunately, the management teams of many organizations become so wrapped up in the thrill of cutting sexy high-powered deals that they often neglect to get the opinion and insights of the foot soldiers and veteran athletes in their company.

Talk about making a huge mistake! As I have pointed out previously, your foot soldiers and veteran athletes are the individuals actually on the front line making your business work. They—not you—ultimately know and control your customers. So either win their support for a proposed deal or risk watching the eventual partnership crumble right before your eyes. The safest and most sensible way to ensure that any potential partnership will work is to try it out within your organization. Set up an informal arrangement and see if there are real synergies and benefits that both companies can reap from working together.

One should think of this preliminary deal-making step as being a lot like a young couple experimenting with living together for a period of time before deciding to tie the knot and get married. Business partnerships are the same way. When they work, they become a true long-term commitment between two parties, not just a one-night, deal-making fling. It's a lot less painful to break off a proposed deal before it has been signed in blood, than to have to publicly admit after the fact that the alliance or partnership turned out to be a relationship from hell. No one ever likes to look like a clueless idiot.

While today's business environment is geared to hyper-decision-making, patience, when applied properly, still pays huge dividends. So have the patience needed. Take the time to see if the synergy and benefits of a prospective deal happen right before your own eyes. Don't become the starry-eyed romantic ready to elope with your new partner at a moment's notice. Prove that your potential deal works out in the field first, as Art Technology's Jeet Singh so clearly states. Then if it does work, you can formalize the relationship later. Better safe than sorry!

JEET SINGH

Founder and Chief Executive
Officer of Art Technology Group

Q **Ragas:** Since cofounding Art Technology Group, your organization has always been focused on building a top-notch sales force. However, your company has also successfully done a number of high-profile alliances. Based on these two experiences, what have you found to be the key to cutting long-lasting deals?

A **Singh:** The most important lesson is, the partnership has to work in the field first. If your salespeople and their salespeople can't sell the partnership, and they don't feel comfortable because they may be stepping on each other's toes, it is never going to work! You can have two CEOs or two CTOs get together and say to each other, "Oh, wow. Our products would work great together!" Then they try to go out and sell this deal, and the salespeople end up stomping on each other because there is some product overlap. You're almost always going to be doing some things that your partner is already doing. However, if the partnership is set up correctly, the salespeople will know how to present the message so that the customer doesn't care there is some overlap, as long as they are getting all the features they want.

Q **Ragas:** So you're saying that your best alliances and partnerships have really happened through first being tried and tested in the sales force. If there are real synergies and benefits being delivered to both companies during this period in the field, then you can always take the potential alliance to a much more formal arrangement. Otherwise, a company just risks spinning its wheels in the deal-making arena!

A **Singh:** Correct. Let your sales force start trying to sell this potential partnership immediately. If there is a favorable response from customers, you should then start moving the deal up through the organization. Once you get to a certain point, obviously both companies will want to provide real resources to market the partnership and start spending money on joint marketing. So when you reach that level, you do then have to cement that relationship at a higher level in both organizations. The vice presidents of both companies should then get together and jointly

decide their budgets on the deal and how much they want to pro-
mote the partnership. But the deals that have really worked best
for us are all with companies whose prod-
ucts and services have sold very effectively without having done any technology
work or marketing materials beforehand.
We didn't even have case studies! So you
can do everything else right, but if you
screw up in the sales force, you're dead in the water!

*"The most impor-
tant lesson is, the
partnership has to
work in the field
first."*

Numbers Don't Matter
If Your Gut Doesn't Feel Right

Once a potential partnership has been proven out in the
field, it is essential for a company to realize that people—
not numbers—really make deals happen. Reaping substantial financial gains from a deal may be great for temporarily
pleasing shareholders or venture capital investors, but numbers shouldn't be the deciding factor in settling upon an
alliance or partnership. When it comes time to decide to
proceed or break off negotiations on a particular deal, I
would actually stick financial incentives at the bottom of the
list. Short-term financial gains mean very little when long-
term, company-building goals are at stake.

Don't ignore your gut instincts, regardless of what a couple of spreadsheet jockeys and a pack of high-priced consultants may be saying. Ask yourself the following gut-check
questions. Do you really trust the people sitting across the
table from you? Would you trust them running your own
business one day? Perhaps most important, does the other
company seem truly committed to building a long-term mutu-
ally beneficial relationship? If the answers to any of these
questions in your mind come back less than satisfactory, then

it's time to pack up your team of lawyers and hyperactive business development people and go home. There will always be other deals to do.

While it might seem trite and downright old-fashioned in a business world moving at a thousand miles an hour, I fully believe that one can never spend enough time getting to know the key players in the organization of a potential partner. Learn their true passions and motivations. Find out what makes them tick. This doesn't mean that you need to make these people honorary members of your family, but it does mean you'll know a lot more about them than just their last names and executive titles when it's time to draft a term sheet or letter of intent. When you cut right to it, business is always personal and chemistry is king.

DAVID MOORE

Chief Executive Officer of 24/7 Media;
Cofounder of Petry Interactive

Q **Ragas:** In the general rush by companies to do deals today, very little thought is given to whether the two organizations share any of the same long-term values, goals, and beliefs. The numbers to do a deal may match up, but below the surface the two companies are largely incompatible. What insights do you have into this and other keys to the deal-making process?

A **Moore:** I think the most important thing in doing any deal is to have real chemistry going with the folks on the other side of the table. You need to find out whether or not you have a good rapport with them and whether or not they're honest and straightforward. Just as important, you need to figure out whether or not you feel the rest of your group can work with them. Try to understand the attitude that they bring to the discussions. If you're comfortable with them and have had a meeting of minds in terms of philosophy, then when you work on the financial end of things it's normally not very hard to come to an agreement. In the end, any deal basically comes down to your gut. Often there are other people within your company that are meeting with these same folks. A lot of times they'll come back after a meeting and say, "Wow, I didn't like them at all." If you don't have a good feeling about a deal, it's almost like being at a bar. You walk up to a girl, and you say, "Hey, you look great tonight." Then she says, "Hey, go take a walk." That's not a good sign. I know I'm being a bit extravagant here, but if you walk up to her and she says, "Hey, I'm fine, but my boyfriend is just coming back from the backroom," that's different. You figure she's already taken or not interested, but she's letting you down easy. In any partnership, you have to get a feel for the people on the other side and make sure that the business reasons are there. Gauge your potential partner's attitude. Is the chemistry really there? Does the deal feel right? Assess this and then decide.

"The most important thing in doing any deal is to have real chemistry going with the folks on the other side of the table."

CHAPTER **12**

SECRETS OF THE SUCCESSFUL IPO

FOR ANY ENTREPRENEUR CRAMPED IN A BASEMENT OR WORKING out of a garage, the three magical letters I-P-O symbolize a glorious light at the end of the tunnel. The initial public offering remains a special reward glittering in the sky for all entrepreneurs working ninety-hour weeks on missions to change the world. While going public should never be viewed as an end game for any entrepreneur or executive, the IPO is indeed the closest thing in modern business to running into the middle of a jungle, pounding one's chest, and crowing, "I've arrived!"

From 1998 until early 2000, going public for the majority of private companies seemed as easy as tying one's shoes in the morning. As long as you had a nice pile of venture capital, a great idea scribbled on a napkin, and truckloads of enthusiasm, Wall Street was ready to welcome your company with open arms. The stock market was in love with potential and what "could be." Then, in April of 2000 the NASDAQ stock market suffered a gut-wrenching collapse. Perception crashed into reality. Almost overnight, a Berlin Wall of epic proportions was erected in IPO land.

This wall sharply divided private companies hoping to IPO into two distinct camps: the performers and the pretenders. The performers were companies with proven business models that either already enjoyed profits or were on the verge of profitability. The pretenders were startups still in need of serious fine-tuning to their business models. As we fast-forward to today, the situation remains much the same. The IPO market remains available only to the most financially sound and already proven digital companies. The border guards on Wall Street don't hesitate to shoot down those pretenders who still try to sneak their way over the wall.

In this chapter I will outline five steps for insuring that your company becomes big and strong enough to climb over this IPO wall. To aid you, CitySearch cofounder Charles Conn and Red Hat founder Bob Young will discuss the importance of taking time and having patience on the path to a successful public offering. Great companies are never built overnight, and a public offering is simply another stepping-stone in the company-building process.

With help from About chief Scott Kurnit and iBeam's Peter Desnoes, we will then look at operational challenges that must be conquered after any IPO. Finally, the key to enjoying any sustainable post-IPO success is to quickly win the faith and trust of your company's new investors. Every post-IPO management team also must become experts at managing investors' expectations, as Exodus Communications founder K. B. Chandrasekhar helps explain.

A Stepping-Stone, Not a Get-Rich-Quick Scheme

First of all, get out of your head any images of luxurious mansions and driving around in exotic sports cars. Any firm really interested in building a sustainable long-term business understands from the beginning that an IPO is simply another stepping-stone in the company-building process. An initial public offering is not a get-rich-quick scheme. What this liquidity event symbolizes is that your company has graduated from the minor leagues into the majors. The outside world now has a stake in your company, and this will create a host of new external as well as internal pressures.

The bygone days of mega-IPOs and gravy times in the tech sector lulled many of us into a flawed fantasyland where we believed that great businesses are built overnight. They aren't. But in a world filled with fast-food windows, ten-minute oil changes, and drive-through pharmacies, it is easy to fall into the trap of believing that great ideas can be turned into great companies in thirty minutes or your money back. We live in a world where it is easy for one's expectations to leap ahead of reality. However, one need only look at the corpses of literally hundreds of failed dot-com companies to see that building great businesses takes time and patience.

Keep this in mind, and it becomes much easier to understand that an initial public offering is simply another stepping-stone in building a business. It is not a reason to check out and head to the beach. Do any of us really believe that Bill Gates would be the richest man in the world today if he had retired from Microsoft after taking the company public in 1986? Of course not! Real wealth creation and sustainable market dominance are generally created after a company goes public. As Red Hat software founder Bob Young quite honestly notes, the way one gets really rich is by building a great company, not flipping a quick IPO.

BOB YOUNG

Founder and Chairman of Red Hat Software

Q **Ragas:** Having already been through the process of taking Red Hat public in an incredibly successful IPO a few years ago, what advice do you have for entrepreneurs and executives who are trying to decide if an IPO should be in their future plans?

A **Young:** When we started, we recognized that we had the opportunity to build a great technology company, but that you can't do this overnight. It is at least a twenty-year process. Our IPO in the summer of 1999 was just year number five in our twenty-year quest. We decided to go public because all revolutions rely on some large capital infusion at some point to take them from the good idea stage to the widely implemented stage. Let me use the American Revolution as an example. George Washington had an army of thirty thousand people who ate a lot of food and used a lot of gunpowder. But who was going to pay for all of this? It was actually the bankers in New England who paid for things. They were every bit as interested in getting away from the dictatorial rules coming from England as patriots like Patrick Henry were! So the American Revolution actually relied on a combination of the patriots and the New England bankers who had the money to finance the war. In Red Hat's case, our IPO was the same sort of partnership. We had the revolutionaries who understood that we had a better way of developing and deploying software, and we had the capital markets who could finance this revolution for us! It's important to understand as a company that an IPO is not an opportunity to get rich. The way you get rich is by building a great company! Some of the recent tech companies that have gone public thought they were all wealthy for a brief period after their

"An IPO is not an opportunity to get rich. The way you get rich is by building a great company."

IPO, but because they didn't actually create any real value, their wealth evaporated very quickly. They weren't bringing real value to their customers.

An IPO Takes Time and Patience

Even with the understanding that building a really great business takes time and patience, there still seems to be this undeniable itch among almost every successful private company to go public. While this is not necessarily a bad thing, it is important to understand that there is very little a company can't accomplish just as well by staying private. In other words, going public won't immediately allow your company to have magical powers that it didn't have before its IPO! In some respects, your organization will actually control its own destiny much less than before you went public, since it now must answer to outside shareholders instead of only company insiders.

While it is true that public companies have the advantage of being able to use their stock as currency for acquisitions, this tactic only works if your company is executing and has a stock that potential buyout targets believe holds real value. If your company is still unproven, you can scratch this advantage of being public right off your list. No one will want your stock. If another one of your company's motivations for going public is that it needs a large capital infusion, then going public is probably the last thing you should be doing. Instead, you should be spending most of you time reassessing if your capital-intensive business model really makes sense in today's profit-conscious marketplace.

The only thing most fledgling young companies succeed in achieving by going public before they are ready is they end up crashing and burning much faster than anyone expected. Either be prepared for the burning heat from investors and the media or sit quietly as a private company for as long as it takes to get your ducks all in a row. Don't rush to place yourself in a situation you can't handle. Once you go public, there's no turning back!

CitySearch cofounder Charles Conn gives a perfect example of a company jumping the gun to go public when he discusses Stamps.com. Without recording any sales, the company was able to IPO in 1999 based on the potential of its proprietary electronic postage technology. However, within a few months of going public, it became clear that Stamps.com's immature business would have serious trouble meeting Wall Street's lofty goals. Investors eventually responded by wiping out over 95 percent of the company's value. Because of this very public belly flop, the company has now been forced to focus almost entirely on survival instead of growth opportunities.

CHARLES CONN

Cofounder and former Chairman of
TicketMaster CitySearch.com

Q **Ragas:** CitySearch was one of the earliest Internet companies to go public, and you've experienced firsthand the ups and downs of being a publicly traded company. When you look back on this entire process, what advice do you have for private companies hoping to one day go public?

A **Conn:** It's so hard to give general advice about the IPO process, because, as you know, it's different every time for everybody. The first thing to remember when you're involved in planning an IPO is that it is very hard to pay attention to the other aspects of your business at the same time. You will likely find yourself completely and utterly consumed by the IPO process for at least four months. The other thing I'd say is to wait and not rush out to try and do an IPO. I think the stock market is now telling people anyway that they have to wait, but there are still lots of companies that go public far too early. Take Stamps.com for example. I really like the people over there, especially former Stamps.com CEO and chairman John Payne. He's really a terrific guy, but Stamps.com went public before it even received approval from the U.S. Postal Service to start selling its electronic postal stamps online. That's just crazy! What happens when you go public is that you trade sophisticated investors who are typically deep pocketed, patient, and intelligent for day traders, doctors, and dentists. These types of smaller investors tend to be more uninformed and impatient.

Q **Ragas:** Well, the days of being able to pull off an IPO by just having an enticing business concept and an impressive group of venture investors are definitely over. In addition, those private companies that do try to go public too early are just opening up a can of worms that can be very hard to close!

A **Conn:** Right. There's no good reason to even be public, except if you need enormous access to capital. If you do, you probably ought to examine your business model again, because it may not be the greatest idea after all. Today, business models that require a lot of capital are not highly favored by the stock market. The only other reason to do an IPO is if you need to make acquisitions. We've used that lever here at CitySearch before, and I think it can be very useful. But you've got to be careful with it. There's no good reason to be public early on in a company's life cycle. Venture investors today typically expect that their companies will go public in a three-to-

"There's no good reason to even be public, except if you need enormous access to capital. If you do, you probably ought to examine your business model again."

five-year time frame. Investors don't expect that you will go public in only a one-year time frame. The only push to go public early on is a decision driven largely by greed, and that's obviously a very bad reason to have for doing anything!

Post-IPO Syndrome

Once a private company does decide that it's time to embark on an IPO, it is crucial that a company's management team understands the cultural impact that a public offering will have on their organization. An initial public offering will fundamentally change the culture of your business for the worse if you allow it. It is key to stress the importance to employees beforehand that an IPO doesn't mean everyone can start showing up at the office at ten in the morning and take two-hour lunch breaks each day. While it might seem ludicrous that any workers might react in this sort of fashion, the fact remains that an IPO can take the edge and hunger out of an organization if you let it.

At this point in the book, I don't have to sit here and tell you that without passion and a feeling of paranoia towards the competition your business can quickly become toast. You already know this. So spread this same message to all of the veterans and foot soldiers throughout your organization that you are continuing to operate like a "raw startup," as About's Scott Kurnit says. Explain to them that an IPO doesn't mean that your company has suddenly reached the top of the mountain and everyone can now go home. If anything, it means that your firm no longer has any hope of flying under the radar. From now on, multiple competitors will be gunning for your market.

Right before and after an IPO are the times when a company can least afford to trip, stumble, or even stub its toe. In fact, your firm must run faster, longer, and harder than it ever has during this period. Immediately shut down any behavior from employees who begin acting like newly minted millionaires in anticipation of your IPO. Remind everyone that those beautiful stock options that they now hold could be in the toilet tomorrow if the company fails to continue executing. Let's face it. Wall Street rewards performers—not pretenders—and post-IPO companies must maintain the same energy as raw startups if they hope to stay on course.

SCOTT KURNIT

Chief Executive Officer and Founder of About, Inc.; former Chief Executive Officer of MCI/News Corp. Internet Ventures

Q **Ragas:** When you look back on your own experience of leading About into the public markets, what are the most fundamental changes that a private company's management team should be prepared to tackle after completing their IPO?

A **Kurnit:** First of all, the IPO process seriously changes a company. The early people who joined your company are often more entrepreneurial than the people who will join your firm post-IPO. That's okay, but it does change your culture. The employees who join a startup early on are prepared to miss a paycheck here and there. However, the people who join post-IPO expect you to have all the cash you need to get profitable. You need your company to run post-IPO just as hard as it did pre-IPO. In some ways, companies really need to make the IPO a non-event. Lots of companies consider it a moment of celebration, but we very consciously did nothing the day of our IPO. I went over and watched our stock trade for the first minute on the NASDAQ and then came back. We had no party or event; it was just business as usual. In reality, our IPO was our fourth round of financing and came after three rounds of private venture financing. After the IPO, I told everyone in our company that we would continue to be running our marathon as a sprint. If they didn't have the energy to do that, then they shouldn't be here. In the tech sector, public companies should realize that they are competing vigorously against private companies that still have all the energy of a raw startup.

"You need your company to run post-IPO just as hard as it did pre-IPO. In some ways, companies really need to make the IPO a non-event."

Companies must continue to have this same raw energy post-IPO if they hope to be successful.

The Rigors of Being Public

The next step in the IPO process is to have your entire organization prepared for the new workload and responsibilities that will come with being a public company. Not only will a firm have to work hard to keeps its organization flowing with the energy of a raw startup post-IPO, but it also must understand beforehand where the responsibilities that come with being public could strain its operations. Appropriate moves must be made beforehand in various departments to insure that the company is capable of dealing with outside shareholders as well as meeting all Securities and Exchange Commission regulations.

An initial public offering isn't some kind of wild party that a company can just sleep off the next day and then forget about. For that matter, an IPO isn't even just a four-to-five month process filled with a bunch of lawyers and bankers and then a road show to cap it all off. When a company decides to go public, it is fundamentally making a long-term commitment to transform its business into a company that must remain largely translucent to the outside world. Just like having a newborn baby, being public will continue to require precious time and resources from your organization long after the day of your IPO party.

Preparing beforehand for the rigor and responsibilities that come with being publicly traded is particularly important for a company's senior management team. Once a company is publicly listed, its senior executives will be expected to frequently play the roles of spokespersons and educators at investment conferences, analysts meetings, and for interactions with the press. Investors, the media—and certainly the SEC—won't want to hear any sob stories that your company was caught off guard by the "surprise demands" that came with being a listed company.

As can easily be imagined, the constant demands to meet Wall Street's financial expectations can frequently cause young post-IPO management teams to feel overwhelmed and strung out. Don't kid yourself into thinking that being public isn't like hopping from the frying pan right into the fire. It certainly is!

Since the responsibilities that come with being a public company can take up a significant part of a senior executive's day, companies should prepare well in advance for these very visible changes, as iBeam's Peter Desnoes makes clear.

PETER DESNOES

Chief Executive Officer and President of iBeam Broadcasting; former Chief Executive Officer of Burnham Broadcasting

Q **Ragas:** Even after the collapse of stock valuations in the tech sector last year, there is still a lot of mystery and intrigue surrounding the IPO process from an outsider's perspective. What is the biggest lesson you learned from taking iBeam public?

A **Desnoes:** For all of my previous experience, I had never run a public company before iBeam. I was told beforehand to make sure that going public was what we really wanted to do, because I would find the process very distracting. My response to this advice was that I was an industrial strength worker, tireless and filled with energy. Now that we've gone public, though, I can tell you there is a very significant part of my day that is spent on one issue or another that is specifically related to being a public company. This means that the hours now devoted to being a public company are taken away from something else that I normally do. We can't even talk to investment analysts now without making public everything we say to them. There are a lot of issues related to being public that are ongoing and challenging. These issues have the ability to materially influence a company's culture as well.

> "There are a lot of issues related to being public that are ongoing and challenging. These issues have the ability to materially influence a company's culture as well."

A company's choice of underwriter for its initial public offering and its ability to properly communicate to the investment community is also extremely important. I've seen a lot of road show presentations by tech companies, and some just don't make a lot of sense. These presentations are not well-articulated and don't differentiate adequately why a company is special and investors ought to put their money at risk. Unless you have a clear differentiating message with a good underwriter, then you are going to have only modest success at best.

Win the Trust of Your New Investors

At this point in the IPO process, let's assume that your once nice and private little company has successfully made its way to the Promised Land. Soak in the splendor for a few days, but don't get carried away with your company's newfound fame and fortune. There's simply no time in the digital business for extended pats on the back. In fact, now that you've been thrust into a kayak that's attempting to brave the rapids of the stock market, there are a few things you should do to make sure you don't get swept over the waterfall.

First of all, it's essential that a newly public company realize that its stock is going to initially seem to the investment world much like the new student on his first day at school—a curiosity that is largely unknown and unproven. With this in mind, it is crucial that the management of any newly public company unbottles the passion it once had as a raw startup and unleashes it all over again. Rediscover this passion for your business, and spread it face-to-face as quickly as possible among the professional investment community.

As I advised in chapter ten on mastering the media, tell your unique compelling story to influential investors, and tell it well. Be clear and to the point about the unique value proposition that your company provides. Explain to the financial media and money managers the notable goals that you have achieved and what new goals you plan to achieve in the future. Then go out and execute on these goals. Build the market's trust. Nothing will build the stock market's confidence quicker in a newly public company than a firm that sets and then consistently meets its goals. Finally, there is also a real art to managing Wall Street's expectations. While you must set sizeable goals for your company and express these goals to investors, you must also make sure that you can always either meet or exceed them. Stay out of forecast cloudland! Consistency breeds trust and is why Exodus founder K. B. Chandrasekhar stresses the importance of quickly building a strong reputation with major investors. As we have seen with the wipeouts of many notable dot-com companies, Wall Street won't hesitate to slaughter a company that breaks its promises.

K. B. CHANDRASEKHAR

Chief Executive Officer and Chairman of Jamcracker Inc.; Founder of Exodus Communications

Q **Ragas:** While the glitter and appeal of doing an initial public offering isn't as bright as it once was, private companies are still eager to tap into the public markets. You enjoyed a very successful IPO with Exodus Communications. What lessons did you take away from this experience?

A **Chandrasekhar:** Entrepreneurs and managers must realize that an IPO is just another event in the life cycle of a company and not the end point. Most companies wrongfully treat an IPO as some kind of end event and then they all close shop and go to the beach. At Exodus Communications, we always viewed the IPO as just another way to get access to a larger equity market, because we always dreamed of Exodus being really big! There are also a lot of responsibilities that come with being a public company, because you are no longer in the hands of a few private investors to whom you can always explain the vagaries of the business.

Q **Ragas:** Right. You're going from having maybe a dozen investors as a private company to an environment as a public company where suddenly you have thousands of investors to keep informed! It's almost like starting from scratch again when it comes to educating your company's investors.

A **Chandrasekhar:** Yes. First and foremost, it is important to educate investors about your company soon after you go public. The second step in this process is to win the trust of a larger number of people, in this case, investors. There is no substitute for proving again and again to investors what you say you are going to do and then going and doing it. The only measure of performance that investors will have about your business is if you deliver or not. Managing expectations is also very important. You must set realistic expectations and then manage these expectations with the public. A company with a multi-billion-dollar valuation with nothing to back up its expectations just doesn't work. The stock market is very smart. The market knows how to give you the opportunity, but it also knows how to pull it away quickly if investors think you can't execute on that opportunity. They also want to see if you are passionate or not about what you do!

"Entrepreneurs and managers must realize that an IPO is just another event in the life cycle of a company and not the end point."

CHAPTER **13**

TRADITIONAL COMPANIES IN THE NEXT ECONOMY

WHAT A DIFFERENCE A FEW YEARS CAN MAKE! ALL THE HYPE ABOUT the Internet has crashed back into reality. Now that the dust has settled and dozens of dot-com companies have not taken over the world (most are buried six feet deep), it's clear that most traditional companies aren't suddenly going to become extinct. Far from it. In fact, if anything, the past two years have seen the blending of "clicks and bricks" as online has met offline. The merger of the old and new has become crucial to achieving sustainable success in the digital world.

Yet for each traditional company that pushes forward with "clicks-and-bricks" initiatives, there are other Old Economy companies giving only lip service to the Internet revolution. These cautious bricks-and-mortar firms often talk a good game to the press, their customers, and their own employees, but behind closed doors they still aren't true believers. After all, from their point of view, with the once cash-rich dot-coms having virtually dried up, there appears to be no immediate threat on the horizon.

On top of this, the market environment is now screaming for earnings, and the launch of a costly new digital initiative is usually the last thing on these executives' minds. But it should be. The Web doesn't have to be a giant cash-sucking black hole for your business. Like it or not, the Internet and wireless technology are not going to disappear anytime soon. Bricks-and-mortar companies can either harness this beast today as a new competitive weapon or watch their competitors use its powers to crush them tomorrow. The choice is theirs.

As I will outline in this final chapter, there are a series of steps that bricks-and-mortar companies can follow to rapidly transform their businesses into true Next Economy leaders without ending up being long-term money losers. Profits and cost savings are definitely readily available on the digital land-scape: One just needs to know how and where to look for them. You don't have to keep stumbling around, trying to find the secrets to Next Economy success. By closely following these steps, a traditional company will be well on its way towards turning its fledgling e-business into a true profit center.

To begin this process, Next Economy leaders Monster.com's Jeff Taylor, Chip Perry of AutoTrader.com, and 1800FLOWERS.com founder Jim McCann will all share their firsthand perspectives on devising the right mindset for approaching the digital business process. Next, we will take a look at organizational sources of inspiration and support for e-business endeavors with Michael Rubin of Global Sports, Macromedia's Rob Burgess, and Intuit's Brooks Fisher. Finally, I will provide three steps for following through on your new digital initiatives with closing insights from Tom Stockham of Ticketmaster, Getty Images chief Jonathan Klein, and MerchantWired's Bob Covington.

Take Advantage of the Current Dot-Coma

There are very few times in business when companies are granted a second lease on life, but this is exactly what is happening to most Old Economy companies with the brutal collapse of the tech sector recently. Even with all of their foot dragging and their outright skepticism surrounding the digital realm, traditional companies are now in a tremendous position to dominate the next generation of the interactive world. With many dot-com companies crippled or non-existent, Old Economy firms now clearly have a unique opportunity to cement their market-leading positions for at least the next decade.

Don't let this opportunity go to waste. Move quickly and decisively. Go digital at all costs. Use this current dot-coma as a unique second chance to add digital capabilities across your business. They will transform your organization into a truly integrated technology-focused company. This means not spinning off the interactive units or divisions of your company into sexy new, stand-alone units. Like it or not, the future of your business is digital. Spinning or carving off these digital assets into a separate operating company will just end up making the eventual reintegration of these same assets that much more difficult.

JEFF TAYLOR

Chief Executive Officer and Founder of
Monster.com and TMP Interactive

Q **Ragas:** The past year has really marked the collapse in valuations or outright failures of numerous pure-play Internet companies. What lessons should bricks-and-mortar companies take away from this experience?

A **Taylor:** My primary lesson is to not carve off your New Economy strategy into a separate company. I watched

Barnes & Noble and Ziff-Davis do this, and I just shook my head. I completely disagree with the concepts of carve-outs for two reasons. It basically takes the life experience of your base business and doesn't allow it to flow freely over into the new business concept. Not only is it ideas that you lose, but it's also the people. By doing a spin-off, you lose the ability to migrate the traditional good thinkers of your business to this New Economy experience. Giving this experience to your existing employees is an incredibly effective way to retain them. Also, if you get the New Economy side of your business growing really strong, there is the risk that your new dot-com employees have no concept of how to run the business. They have no experience. They only know how to leverage some of the tools and some of the services that the Internet provides, but they don't know how to actually run the core business. So everybody loses! What we've seen now for the most part is that when the online and offline businesses are separated, neither one really has much of a chance.

"There are very few times in business when you get a reprise and actually have a period of time where your competitors completely back off after they were just about to crush you."

Q **Ragas:** In other words, carving off the Internet unit of your traditional company is a lot like shooting yourself in the foot. To prosper, these two entities have to act like vital organs that really need to be inside the same body to survive. One can't function effectively without the other!

A **Taylor:** Yes. I also think the "dot-coma" we are seeing right now is very real. This is very relevant for bricks-and-mortar companies. There are very few times in business when you get a reprise and actually have a period of time where your competitors completely back off after they were just about to crush you. I think that's kind of the "dot-coma" stage that we are in now, where Old

Economy companies actually have the ability to take a breath and say, What did I miss last year? I think it should be the Old Economy companies' absolute mission to break their businesses right now. This is what I call evolutionary versus revolutionary. This is Deming versus Darwin. For the last fifty years, we've been focused in on Deming and improving our product or service's quality through evolutionary changes to improve our business. But it's now time to be more Darwinian and realize that this is survival of the fittest. We now have this little break where the dotcoms have three flat tires and have to pull over to the side of the road to get pumped up again. It may not be this first group of companies that come back out and beat the Old Economy companies, but there will be another wave after them.

Should You Web-Enable or Do a Digital Endowment?

Once your company is truly ready to wholeheartedly attack the digital opportunity, it becomes important to assess which of two paths your organization is best equipped to travel. This decision will largely revolve around the core assets and competencies of your business, how they apply to the digital realm, and the level of risk your organization is willing to take. In other words, is your business most interested in Web-enabling its existing business, or is it more interested in leveraging its existing traditional assets to create an entirely new digital business?

Offline retailers like The Gap and Barnes & Noble have done an excellent job at Web-enabling their online businesses by providing their customers the option of purchasing their products over the Web. On the other hand, software firm Macromedia decided to leverage the existing popularity of its Web design tools into an entirely new entertainment company called Shockwave.com. Enron

Corporation utilized its existing core competencies in commodities trading to develop an entirely new commodities e-marketplace in EnronOnline.

The first step in deciding which of these paths your firm should take is to compose a detailed checklist of your company's core assets and core competencies. Then take time to review this list and begin crafting with various departments of your organization how these assets and competencies could be creatively applied to the digital realm. You will then have a much clearer idea of what you should do, and you can make the choice whether to Web-enable your existing business or offer up a digital endowment for an entirely new e-business.

CHIP PERRY

Chief Executive Officer and
President of AutoTrader.com;
former Vice President of the Los Angeles Times

Q **Ragas:** Clearly, every offline company today must establish some type of online beachhead. So what firsthand advice do you have for traditional bricks-and-mortar companies that have only dipped their toes into the online waters?

A **Perry:** There are two different paths that bricks-and-mortar companies can take. One path is to leverage the Internet to enhance the company's existing business. This means offering things like online availability and online marketing of a company's current product set. Home Depot is a good example of a traditional company that is moving pretty aggressively in that direction. Another example is Toys "R" Us, which has partnered online with Amazon.com to run its online toy business. These companies are looking to simply "Web-enable" their physical company. However, I think the angle that has the best potential for massive new value creation is to create an entirely new business that leverages your offline assets, not just tries to enhance them. That's essentially what we've done here with AutoTrader.com. I like to describe this process as receiving a wonderful endowment from our three main offline owners. But the tricky part of having an endowment is to not receive baggage along with the endowment. Baggage comes in the form of constraints on how your company develops, markets, and sells your new digital products. Anytime you get an endowment, you have to think about what the baggage is that you might inherit along with it!

Q **Ragas:** So for bricks-and-mortar companies to succeed by heading down this somewhat riskier second path, they must be willing to truly let their new digital creations run freely and not be handicapped with operational restrictions.

A **Perry:** Choosing this angle is all about creating an entirely new business, while leveraging the bricks-and-mortar company's offline assets. For instance, if I had tried to create AutoTrader.com inside the newspaper industry, I would have been subject to a lot of baggage. I wouldn't have been able to approach the best advertising customers of the newspaper alone. I would have had to have the newspaper's sales representatives with me, and they would have wanted to package my product in with theirs. I would never have had enough autonomy to really get wings and fly! Traditional companies must decide which fork in the road they want to go down. If they choose the endowment angle, they have to give the new business a chance to succeed—they must be careful they don't apply any baggage that weighs it down. That's the problem with a lot of these newly created startups formed by bricks-and-mortar companies. The Internet team is often not given the clear shot it needs to create a dramatically superior product or service.

"The angle that has the best potential for massive new value creation is to create an entirely new business that leverages your offline assets."

Pay Up or Partner

Before choosing whether to Web-enhance their business or do an endowment, traditional companies must fully understand that the days of building effective online and wireless projects on a shoestring budget are gone. In a market environment filled with incredible clutter, even the most innovative bricks-and-mortar companies have had to pay big to play online. The front and back end technologies and the in-house technical team needed to maintain a dynamic corporate site today are sizeable. Be prepared either to give your interactive efforts the resources and budget needed to really survive and thrive, or don't even start them in the first place.

Customers and suppliers expect to receive the same level of service and quality over the Web as they have always received offline. Perhaps the biggest risk that bricks-and-mortar firms face in taking up interactive initiatives is to do more harm than good to their existing brands. Don't ever risk tarnishing the reputation and reliability of your brand because of a half-baked Web initiative that leaves customers, suppliers, and the media with a nasty taste in their mouths. You only get one chance to make a first impression, so get it right the first time. Come out of the gates with a digital strategy that has the budget and the resources needed to win the race.

JIM McCANN

Founder, Chairman, and
Chief Executive Officer of 1800FLOWERS.com

Q **Ragas:** What do you believe are the biggest obstacles traditional companies must overcome in the interactive world and what are some of the steps that these companies must take to be successful online?

A **McCann:** The opportunity today to bring a business inexpensively to the Net is over. That window is closed. When we first went online in 1992, it was inexpensive to create an interactive business. But customer expectations have risen, and the cost of actually being able to build a Web site with scalability is now much higher. It's not an inexpensive proposition anymore! Companies also must realize that their Web initiative will typically grow slower than they expect and cost more than they think. I think those are two rules that we found true with our "most conservative" projections. For example, we built our first Web site for $50,000! I don't know anyone who creates a Web site now who gets into the game for under a million dollars. In addition, if you already have a big brand, you really can't go cheap, because you need scalability for your site to be able to handle customer demand. Because of how expensive this business has become, you are now seeing a number of partnerships. A company like ours, that has already spent well over $100 million dollars on our online efforts from a technology point of view, now has a number of brand name companies approach us about partnerships. Companies are now realizing that they have to be on the Web, but it could be a $20- to $100-million proposition to try and do it all on their own!

> *"Customer expectations have risen, and the cost of actually being able to build a Web site with scalability is now much higher."*

Can You Afford to Be a One-Man Web Band?

Once you have committed to either Web-enabling your existing business, launching an entirely new e-business, or developing a combination of the two, your traditional company should begin contemplating potential e-partnerships. Take a long hard look at the digital blueprint in front of you and decide if various portions of this emerging business would be best served by partnering with other companies. For example, after fumbling with its own Web plans for well over a year, Toys "R" Us ultimately decided to partner with Amazon.com. The e-tailing giant now handles all site development, customer service, and order fulfillment for ToysRUs.com.

In similar fashion, the majority of Fortune 500 firms have now decided to partner with B-to-B leaders Commerce One and Ariba, instead of developing their own e-marketplace and procurement solutions. Clearly, while partnerships and alliances are nothing new for bricks and mortar firms, the pace and number of them needed to succeed in the Next Economy is an exponential increase over the traditional business environment. The best advice in tackling the Web is to keep one's core competencies in-house and outsource the rest. Break free from the offline mentality of being a one-man Web band. Now is not the time to try and reinvent the wheel!

MICHAEL RUBIN

Founder, Chairman, and
Chief Executive Officer of Global Sports

Q **Ragas:** You've been able to transition your company from a traditional bricks-and-mortar retailer into an e-commerce infrastructure provider for the sporting goods industry. Based on this experience, what advice do you have for other offline companies looking to devise an effective digital strategy?

A **Rubin:** The first thing traditional companies need to realize is that they actually have a number of great advantages for succeeding online. They already have a brand name and proven marketing power. That is a big portion of what all of the dot-com pure-play companies are trying to create. So the real question for bricks-and-mortar companies becomes, how do you build a successful Internet strategy that leverages these existing assets? Companies should evaluate their situations and see how big the opportunity is online and how they can create the best return. A lot of the CEOs of big companies thought they could just go out and spend a lot of money and do it on their own, while maybe creating a financial arbitrage opportunity in the stock market.

Q **Ragas:** Right. The days of traditional companies simply slapping together a Web strategy in hopes of boosting their stock price and exciting shareholders are history. But that doesn't make the Net any less important for them. Customers and suppliers still expect to have the Net available to them as a sales, distribution, and procurement platform.

A **Rubin:** I think what these traditional companies need to do is to find a creative way to leverage their assets online. This could mean that they do it all themselves, but they can also find other people to help them go online. We help people to go online in the sporting goods category, although partnering isn't necessarily always the best path to online success. Someone like clothing retailer The Gap has done very well online on its own. However, a lot of companies that thought the way to succeed online was to do things alone are now beginning to partner. It really depends on the unique situation of each bricks-and-mortar company.

> *"A lot of companies that thought the way to succeed online was to do things alone are now beginning to partner."*

Get Some Geeks!

The next step in the digital transformation of a traditional company is to properly leverage the existing tech-savvy human capital in your organization. Usually, the best new e-business ideas don't originate in a wood-paneled boardroom, but instead come from the foot soldiers sitting in the cramped cubicles of the corporation. Yes. The geeks. What?

You certainly didn't forget that you have them, right? I'm talking about the invaluable legions of techies that every large established company must have but is afraid to confer with on business matters. Big mistake.

Rewin their trust. Burn your outdated org charts right in front of your geeks if need be, but get them involved in your high-level digital planning process. Listen to their insights and suggestions on the development of the interactive terrain. If you're like most bricks-and-mortar companies, not everything they're going to tell you is going to make you smile, but try to appreciate their sometimes brutally honest advice. Unlike a high-priced consultant who may only be a corporate cheerleader, geeks grew up with the Web. Respect what they think.

Now, this doesn't mean worshipping everything that your geeks have to say. It's just that their advice is likely to be more pure and unfiltered than the carefully worded dribble of some office-politics-conscious, mid-level manager. As I've stressed throughout this book, honesty is king on the Web, and receiving unbiased thoughts on the future of your company's digital direction is invaluable information to have at hand. Filter it as best you can to separate the geeks' fanciful 2001: A Space Odyssey chatter from the current digital reality, and you will likely have the beginnings of a very powerful clicks-and-bricks brew.

ROB BURGESS

Chairman and Chief Executive Officer of Macromedia; former Senior Vice President of Silicon Graphics

Q **Ragas:** Numerous traditional companies seem to have trouble envisioning the new opportunities the Net and emerging technologies can provide for their businesses. Where should bricks-and-mortar companies turn for sources of digital strategy inspiration?

A **Burgess:** The way traditional companies tend to run is that they listen almost exclusively to their senior people who have been around for a long time. That's a bad idea. One of the biggest things I tried to do when I joined Macromedia was to listen to the people who were "of" and "from" the Internet. So you find yourself listening to a twenty-five-year-old or a twenty-two-year-old instead of a forty-five-year-old. Bricks-and-mortar companies need to learn to ignore the organizational charts when they decide to go online. In fact, I have never published an organization chart. Our hierarchy, what there is of it, is in the background. Who works for whom shouldn't matter! Even if you have two hundred people that work for you, you don't have a God-given right to make decisions. I think the people that should get to make decisions are the people that know the most, regardless if they happen to be a manager or not! Some people are really good at making decisions, but they're not really good at being a manager. Some people are great at getting the best out of others, but they aren't good decision makers. So companies must allow themselves to be led in new areas by people who actually "live" in the digital medium.

> *"Bricks-and-mortar companies need to learn to ignore the organizational charts when they decide to go online. Who works for whom shouldn't matter!"*

Q **Ragas:** Clearly, traditional bricks-and-mortar companies can learn a lot by listening to employees in their organization who live, eat, and breathe the digital world. However, isn't there a risk to digesting every business idea that they suggest?

A **Burgess:** It's not a unilateral thing. You have to listen to them, but then you also must apply the wisdom of the people who are acquainted with running the overall business. That said, it's important to get some geeks! If you don't have someone that works in your office with purple hair, you're going to have trouble.

A television commercial that I really love is the one for the online brokerage firm Ameritrade. It is about Stewart, a young mailroom guy with dyed hair who is teaching his boss how to trade online. It's totally right! These Stewarts understand the Net, and they're not corrupted and biased by all the stuff the older people know. Traditional companies absolutely must get some employees around them who really understand the medium. Remember, get some geeks!

You Need Support from the Top Brass

After you have successfully outlined a promising digital strategy with insights from your geeks, the next step is to build consensus at the highest levels of your organization. From the offices of the CEO and the board of directors to every divisional and departmental head, the entire company must be 100 percent focused on the mission to "go digital or die." There must be no alternatives offered. For any bricks-and-mortar firm trying to transition into a Next Economy company, there can be no dissension in the ranks surrounding the digital blueprint that has been developed.

As I discussed in chapter nine on hyper-growth management, one of the keys to implementing serious change in a traditional business environment is for an entire organization to preach and believe the new hyper-change religion that it has created. It might sound like a page out of a cult leader's handbook, but the bricks-and-mortar company must rally behind the new mantra and believe every word of it. The only way for this to happen is for all of the top brass to believe wholeheartedly in the new mission. Leaders lead and followers follow. Every company works that way.

A fractious organization is the last thing any transitioning company needs as it launches a new digital strategy. Nip in the bud any cult leaders spewing their own flavor of e-strategy religion, or run the risk of an uncommitted organization for this enormous change. Trying to get a company to break its old habits and march down unproven new paths is never easy, but with the backing of the top brass and a realistic new fighting song to march to, a firm's foot soldiers are capable of doing amazing things. Never underestimate the power of building support from the top down.

BROOKS FISHER

Vice President, Strategic Initiatives of Intuit; former Vice President of Infoseek

Q **Ragas:** Many offline companies have trouble figuring out how to get the ball rolling on an effective Internet strategy. You've been through this entire process with the launch of Quicken.com for Intuit. What lessons have you learned along the way?

A **Fisher:** The first thing companies must do is to develop a simple strategy that is bought all the way up to the board of directors' level. When you are trying to change, it's more difficult to do in an environment where you already have success. There's no burning platform, and there's no crisis, so you have to take highly successful people who are really good at what they do and essentially tell them you want them to do something different. That's always difficult. There is natural resistance to this, because these people are typically smart, effective, and capable. If you don't have their absolute firm support all the way up to the CEO and board of directors, you're going to end up spinning your wheels, because their lack of support will cycle back to the foot soldiers in the trenches.

Q **Ragas:** So, to have any chance, this new digital strategy must first receive backing from the top brass. But how do you build this company-wide consensus for something that is entirely new and unfamiliar and seemingly breaks the organization's existing habits?

A **Fisher:** The primary thing is to get clarity in very simple terms at the highest level. At Intuit, we had a successful business, but it was flattening out. We had a very simple mission to figure out how to get these businesses into a connected environment. It was very much a situation where the future of the company was at stake. Those who had tremendous experience knew that they had to be as supportive and cooperative as possible. There wasn't any lack of enthusiasm or support from our employees, but you're still bouncing against behavior. You had a company in our case that was absolutely the best in the world at figuring out what customers wanted and managing an annual release cycle for desktop software. That's great, but how do you take this same group of people and get them to put out a new Web product in six weeks, and it's going to change again every three months? That's hard. I even had very capable software engineers sit down and say to me that certain Web site plans just couldn't be done. I had to say simply, "This is the assignment." You are dealing with a level of ambiguity that means you're making decisions with less specificity around what the risks are. Companies have to do that to succeed online. They have to be willing to make some mistakes and go back and undo them!

> *"When you are trying to change, it's more difficult to do in an environment where you already have success."*

The Day of Integration Is Near

As you build support in your organization for these new digital initiatives from the top down, it is important to remember that the days of sticking a small digital S.W.A.T. team into some lonely corner of your monolithic corporation are done. The last thing any bricks-and-mortar company should be doing at this point is developing an entirely separate unit or department that focuses exclusively on interactive and digital projects. You have to think of your online and wireless initiatives as a new type of secret sauce that needs to be spread throughout the entire organization and not kept locked up in a room somewhere.

If this secret sauce is going to be effectively spread throughout a traditional business, the company's management team must find ways to relate the new digital initiatives to past "company-changing" experiences. Obviously, while the Internet and wireless technology have been incredible paradigm shifters for traditional business, they are far from the only events that have forced entire businesses to drastically rework themselves. Find similar challenges within your business that employees have conquered in years past, and everyone will do a better job of relating to the possibilities and challenges that the digital world has brought.

TOM STOCKHAM

President of Access and Emerging Markets at Ticketmaster; former General Manager of CitySearch

Q **Ragas:** Often, traditional bricks-and-mortar companies seem to have trouble in getting their entire organization to "buy into" their new digital initiatives. What advice do you have for firms struggling to spread the "digital gospel" throughout their organizations?

A **Stockham:** The key early challenge is to get as many people as possible to relate to whatever the new digital business is that you are creating. One of our biggest challenges early on with Ticketmaster.com was that most people just thought of the

Internet as this "new, new thing." They didn't think of it as a new distribution channel like the telephone was for Ticketmaster almost a decade ago. When you get people to relate to previous company-wide experiences, you can help demystify the new thing. The definite pattern to failure for a company is to get only a couple of people thinking about what you are trying to do and everyone else feeling like they can't relate to it. If you're a big organization, you want all of your bright people focused on how to make this new thing work. This doesn't mean asking everyone to lead your new electronic initiatives, but you need to make sure that everyone begins to associate this new thing with company experiences that they are familiar with! One of the reasons that the Internet didn't make us panic was we already had tackled similar challenges and knew how to overcome them.

Q **Ragas:** So one of the very early steps for traditional companies laying the groundwork for a digital strategy is to find ways to get the entire organization to relate to the new challenges.

A **Stockham:** I've found that companies must have a healthy internal group who can go out and try new things. Three out of four of a company's new initiatives may end up being failures, but the key is for companies to find ways to quickly adopt the new things that are successful. That's a challenge for any business virtually all of the time. People generally don't understand when the business that they've helped to start gets turned over nor how they turn it over within their organization. For example, we're now coming up on almost 30 percent of all Ticketmaster's overall sales volume coming from Ticketmaster.com. We're growing incredibly fast, and one day we are going to wake up and most of Ticketmaster's business is going to be electronically enabled.

"The key early challenge is to get as many people as possible to relate to whatever the new digital business is that you are creating."

In other words, if companies haven't figured out how to make the transition and to eventually have a healthy integration with the parent company, then all that great growth you experienced is going to crash in the other direction. The lesson that everyone in the bricks-and-mortar world needs to learn is to understand what happens when their Internet unit actually becomes a majority of their overall business!

Be Prepared for the Results

As your new digital initiatives become fully operational throughout your organization, it is vital that the company continues to over-allocate the amount of internal resources needed to sustain this "go digital or die" mantra. Forget about taking any breaks. This is pedal-to-the-metal time! If you really have found sensible ways to use the Web and wireless to improve the customer experience and your business processes, then growth will be the least of your worries. The biggest challenge will be building, and then maintaining, the company-wide support needed to keep these new digital initiatives operating at peak levels of performance.

As I mentioned earlier, the risks of tarnishing a bricks-and-mortar company's brand in the interactive world are very real—but can be easily avoided by planning ahead. It is sensible to expect revolutionary rather than evolutionary growth in all of your current and future projects. With this expectation, the traditional company will be prepared to under-promise and over-deliver to key customers, suppliers, investors, and the media from day one. As Getty Images chief Jonathan Klein notes, the pace of rapid technology adaptation is poised to significantly quicken, and digital technologies will become increasingly pervasive over the coming years.

JONATHAN KLEIN

President and Chief Executive Officer of Getty Images

Q **Ragas:** Your company was very early in realizing how the Internet could fundamentally revolutionize your business. What lessons do you have for other companies attempting to migrate a bricks-and-mortar business to the Web?

A **Klein:** What I think is most important to recognize is that the Web does not work for all offline businesses. A company needs to look closely at its products or services and customer base and ask itself some simple questions. Am I going to use the Internet to change my method of marketing, or am I going to use it to change my method of distribution? Are those changes going to benefit customers so they can use my product or service more easily and more quickly? The objective of moving a business from an offline to an online environment must be to make it better for your customer, because, if it is better for your customer, you will do better! Not every product or service lends itself well to the Internet. In the case of Getty Images, we were very fortunate in that the Internet is perfectly suited for the distribution of intellectual property, because pictures can be transmitted online digitally in real time. Very few products can be moved from a supplier to a customer literally in real time and online. Most of the best known e-commerce companies cannot actually fulfill an order online. They send it by FedEx or UPS. It arrives at the customer's door in much the same way it has for a hundred years!

Q **Ragas:** Yes. For some offline companies' products and services, the harsh reality is that the Web does not always offer a superior customer purchasing experience. Let's assume, though, that a company's product or service does lend itself to the Net. What step should come next in the process?

A **Klein:** Once you've decided that your product or service lends itself to the Web, the next question to ask yourself is, how quickly? Everyone knows that with most major technological developments it is not a matter of whether they'll happen, but when they'll happen. As soon as people began using cellular phones, we knew that there would be a point in time when everyone would be using some form of cellular telephony. As soon as people started using microwave ovens, we knew they would cease to be a luxury item over time and that everyone would have one. I think the same applies to different industries and definitely to the Web. For Getty Images, it was never a question of "would our customers use the Web to buy pictures." We never struggled with that question. We knew that they would. The question we really had was related to the pace of this adoption. The lesson that we've learned from this experience is that customers adopt new technologies more quickly than you think. Adoption is seldom evolutionary, but often revolutionary. So be prepared for this rapid adoption curve.

"Customers adopt new technologies more quickly than you think."

Trust Your Instincts

Perhaps the final and most valuable piece of advice for any bricks-and-mortar company on a quest to go digital is, trust your instincts. Seek outside advice, but don't ignore your gut. While this seems so logical, the reality is that many bricks-and-mortar companies have convinced themselves that they are utterly clueless in the digital world. This simply isn't the case. The digital world should only intimidate those companies that have lousy business fundamentals in the first place. While the Web and wireless represent a new playing field for business, the rules of the game haven't changed.

No one is ever going to understand your business and know your customers better than you do—not even your closest competitors. Knowing this, you will almost always be at a distinct advantage over an outside advisor as to what digital initiatives make the most sense. So have confidence and conviction behind your opinions on how the digital terrain will develop in your industry. Don't believe everything that you hear. Just because a high-priced consulting shop might know the latest buzzwords doesn't mean they understand the inner workings of your corporation.

ROBERT COVINGTON

Chief Technology Officer and
Executive Vice President of MerchantWired

Q **Ragas:** Many traditional companies still don't really know where to begin when devising a digital business strategy. Many times, they seem to end up with a jumbled array of disjointed Web initiatives. So what lessons do you have to share with bricks-and-mortar companies?

A **Covington:** The foremost lesson for succeeding online is a very simple thing that every legacy business should do, which is: Listen to your customers. In our particular case, the concept for MerchantWired started back in 1997 when I was with Simon Property Group, the largest retail real estate company in North America. We were talking to our retailers and they told us they wanted to integrate their virtual and physical stores, but they had a problem. MerchantWired was born because these storeowners couldn't get reliable networking to their stores. By taking the time to listen to what your customers are saying, a bricks-and-mortar company can tailor a new technology solution that will eventually succeed, as opposed to trying out some crazy concepts and waiting to see what catches on. Your customers will almost always tell you what they want!

Q **Ragas:** Customers are definitely a great launching pad for uncovering new market opportunities, although I sense that many bricks-and-mortar companies are afraid to trust their instincts on the Net. Instead, they end up relying all too often on outside advice.

A **Covington:** One of the problems that many legacy companies have is they don't want to trust their own instincts in the New Economy. I often see traditional companies being led astray by consultants telling them they don't know what they are doing in the digital world. In many cases, these traditional companies should just trust their instincts. There are new things to learn in the New Economy, but there are also reasons why legacy companies are already successful. They're not a six-month-old startup. They've been around for a long time and know how to do business. Just because some rules are changing doesn't necessarily mean that all rules are gone. There are many rules of business that simply never change and still need to be closely adhered to in the New Economy! So while legacy companies need to think outside the box, they must not forget the elements of the legacy business that have made them successful so far!

"There are many rules of business that simply never change and still need to be closely adhered to in the New Economy!"

INDEX

A

About.com, successful customer grabbing by, 109
Accounting department, sales hat worn by, 81
Acquisitions to employ fast-follower strategy, 136
Ad agency fees, 74
Advertising campaign, mistake of creating big, 74
Age of Commoditization, 86–89
Alliances. *See also* Partnerships
chemistry in, 203–205
creating successful, 68, 69, 190–205
media attention used to create, 187

unbreakable, 190–191
Amazon.com
customer loyalty to, 113, 114
initial targeted brand of, 97
personalized recommendations of, 28
reason for great brand name today of, 89–90, 91, 93, 96
Toys 'R Us partnership with, 229–230
warp-speed growth and subsequent trouble of, 164
America Online (AOL)
as being good at marketing, 70
as best rather than first in category, 124
customer loyalty to, 113